PRAISE FOR *GIRLZ 'N THE HOOD*

"Mary Hill-Wagner's *Girlz 'n the Hood: A Memoir of Mama in South Central Los Angeles* is sometimes hilarious, sometimes painful, yet always centered in the reality of her early life with her mother, Sarah Gordon, and her brothers and sisters."

— Professor Leon Dash, author of *Rosa Lee: A Generational Tale of Poverty and Survival in Urban America*

"There are many stories which comprise the history of Black Americans. *Girlz 'n the Hood* is a wonderful, warm memoir that helps us put together a critical piece of L.A. A wonderful read."

— Nikki Giovanni, poet

GIRLZ 'N THE HOOD

A Memoir of Mama in South Central Los Angeles

Dr. Mary Hill-Wagner

Pact Press

Published by Pact Press
An imprint of
Regal House Publishing, LLC
Raleigh, NC 27612
All rights reserved

https://pactpress.com

Printed in the United States of America

ISBN -13 (paperback): 9781646030781
ISBN -13 (epub): 9781646031030
Library of Congress Control Number: 2020948459

Interior and cover design by Lafayette & Greene
Cover images © by C. B. Royal

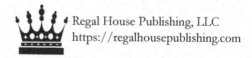

Regal House Publishing, LLC
https://regalhousepublishing.com

The following is a work of creative nonfiction. The events are portrayed to the best of Mary Hill-Wagner's memory. While all the stories in this book are true, some names and identifying details have been changed or have been eliminated to protect the privacy of the people involved and to minimize harm.

Printed in the United States of America

To Mama, who wanted to;
to Ellerbe, who said I could;
to Clancy, who said I must;
to Andrea, who believed in it;
to Geoff, who did the same;
and to my beloved Marcus,
who made it all possible.

A NOTE FROM THE AUTHOR:

Memory has its own story to tell. I have tried to recreate events, locales, and conversations from my memories of them. I have retold them in a way that evokes the feeling and meaning of what was said in all instances, the essence of the dialogue is accurate.

ONE

Mama Throws a Party

My mother was plotting murder at the kitchen table. Again.

"You shouldn't put up with this bullshit, Pat," my mother said. "Just get yourself a big boilin' pot and wait for that son of a bitch to go to sleep. Put that pot on nice and long and put in a little lye. Go in. Shake the bed so he knows it's you, and dump that shit over his lyin', wife-beatin', cheatin'-ass head."

I stood in the kitchen on the red Carnation milk crate. I tried to keep the dishes from clattering and clanging. But I just knew that my mother was going to glance over, notice my seven-year-old self, and yell something about getting out of grown folks' business. I knew that as soon as they started discussing Pat's husband, Gene, I was supposed to excuse myself and leave the room. It was risky to keep doing the dishes, but I wanted to hear what happened.

Even though I was doing the dishes as I was supposed to, I wouldn't have been surprised if she'd kicked the crate from under me and let my head hit the tile floor, just to teach me a lesson about snooping. My mother didn't like kids getting all up in grown folks' conversation.

Pat said, "But I cain't. I just cain't. You know I love that man. And he say he real sorry."

"You is a simple-ass bitch," my mother said to her best friend in the world. "You gonna get enough of not listenin' to what I'm sayin'. I hope I don't have to go to yo' funeral or send that good-for-nothin' man to his."

Pat was a very tall woman who could reach anything on

top of the refrigerator without getting up on her tiptoes. Now, she sat in one of the flowered, padded dinette chairs with her long brown arms draped over the back. She could almost reach to the floor. Her wig seemed to be on sideways. Her apple-red lipstick was smeared and her eyes were blood-shot.

My mother got up and went over to the refrigerator, reached in, and got out a red Popsicle. She handed it to her friend. Pat held it against the knot over her right eye.

"You know what I been tellin' you. I told you and told you that that man was going to raise his hands to you one day. Remember? When you told me that he couldn't keep his Johnson in his pants and he was running around with every little ho in that pagan-ass church you go to, I said, 'a man that will cheat on his woman will beat on his woman.' I know you remember when I said that shit. And I said back then that you should put a cap in his ass or leave him. I told you those was yo' choices."

I thought about sending up a wish and crossing my fingers so they would be sure not to notice me. But it's hard to do dishes with crossed fingers. And if my mother discovered the dishes weren't done—in addition to the fact that I was snooping—well, I would get a wake-up whuppin'. Those were the worst kind because you couldn't even pretend to outrun the blows when you were asleep.

Pat pushed her big body away from the table and scratched the chair loudly on the floor. She smoothed down her sun-dress that had giant daisies on it. The dress barely covered her bottom. She tried to set her wig to rights but it still hung crooked.

"I gotta go get dinner on, Say," she said, using her pet name for my mother. "I'll call you later."

Pat came over to me and handed me the Popsicle. I took it, although I was still pretending to be invisible. I set the Popsicle on the counter and finished the dishes.

My mother stood and accepted a hug from Pat.

I climbed down from the crate awkwardly with the Popsicle in my hand. I tried to tiptoe out of the kitchen past my mother. My mother grabbed the back of my collar.

My mother stood over me like a large dog, but instead of whipping me she just said, "Don't you tell nobody what we been talkin' 'bout up in here. You hear? We don't need to add gossip to your sins. You hear me, girl?"

"Yes, ma'am," I mumbled.

The next day all was forgotten as far as I could see. The whole house was in an uproar because Uncle Lo' was getting out of jail. I still don't know why it was made out to be such a big deal when he got out. Uncle Lo' always seemed to be getting out of one jail or another.

Uncle Lo' ducked as he came in through the front door. His real name was Lorenzo Gordon Senior, but everyone seemed to think it was really funny to call him Lo'. He was even taller than Pat. He could see the top of the refrigerator all the way to the back. His head was shaved so he was bald now. He'd grown a pencil mustache. It stood out on his caramel-colored lip. He said it made him look like Earl Flynn, whoever that was.

Uncle Lo' was carrying his usual can of Schlitz Malt Liquor—a 16-ounce can because an 8-ounce can of anything was for "guys with sugar in their shoes."

His wife, Annette—who was almost as tall as our living room picture window and just about as wide—broke through the crowd of children and adults in the tiny living room and threw her arms around him. We called her Ainey because Aint Annette was too hard to say. Uncle Lo' put his massive hands over Ainey's butt.

"Annette, I got your present right here," Uncle Lo' said as he pushed Ainey up against him.

"Y'all keep that smut for later. Boy, get your ass in here and say hello to your big sister," my mother said.

"Tank! How the hell did I miss you standin' over there," Uncle Lo' said, giving my mother a huge hug and a smooch on the cheek. "I met a couple of guys in the joint I might want to introduce you to."

"Boy, don't nobody want your jailbird-ass friends," my mother said, and everyone laughed loudly. And somebody brought out a few cases of beer and bottles of I.W. Harper whiskey. The grown-ups started flowing out onto the back porch. The kids got plopped in front of the TV. *Gunsmoke* was on. Only I went out after the adults.

"Girl, what the hell you think you doin'?" my mother said. "I ain't no fool. You just want to get all up in grown folk conversation."

"I...I...just want to see if anybody want some ice or something," I said.

My mother looked down at me and raised her hand. But just before any blow could be struck, Uncle Lo' lifted me up onto his lap and hugged me against his wall-like chest. I could see my mother over his right shoulder.

"What's wrong with you, Tank? I don't want to hear no cryin' babies. Cryin' babies is sad. And I ain't had nothin' but sad for six months," Uncle Lo' told her and started to tickle me as he carried me onto the back porch. I laughed so much I almost peed.

"Lo', you gonna spoil her," my mother said. Then she crossed the room and planted her bulk in a folding chair. She took out a pack of roll-your-own cigarettes, tapped some tobacco into the paper, and licked the cigarette shut. She lit it, shook the match out, and dropped it on the stone floor. Throwing her left arm across her massive chest, she propped up her cigarette hand and puffed away.

I sat on Uncle Lo's lap like I had done a hundred times before. I closed my eyes, and sucking on two fingers, pretended to fall asleep.

"Where's my new brother-in-law? Who is it this week, Say?" my Uncle Lo' asked. My head bounced on his chest as he laughed.

"You know what, Lo'? You can go fuck yourself," my

mother said. "You know that me and Big Willie still together."

"Oh yeah, he's the *one* I like. He didn't want to come to my homecoming?"

"He just ain't here right now," my mother said. "I told his sorry ass to spend a few days at his mama's house befo' I had to kill a motherfuckah up in here."

"Why? What did you do to this one?" Uncle Lo' said.

"I didn't do nothin' to him. That sorry-ass man spent the rent money. And do you know what he spent it on?"

"Wine, women, and song," Uncle Lo' said. "'Cause that's damn sure what I would spend it on."

I loved it when he got poetic.

"No, that man got eight babies up in this house, and I don't care if only two is his. It's still eight babies, and he spent the rent money on pitchin' pennies. Can you imagine usin' up your whole paycheck pitchin' some damn pennies? You know that stupid-ass game where a bunch of sorry-ass niggas stand around and pitch pennies at a wall, and they see who gets closest? And whatever idiot gets closest, he wins all the damn pennies. And sometimes they don't pitch just pennies, they use dimes and even quarters. But they still calls it pitchin' pennies."

"Do you know how long you have to play that shit 'fo you lose your whole damn paycheck? I'll tell you—all damn weekend long, that's how long. And he always up in my grill 'bout not working. He don't want me to use my nursing license to go back to work, talkin' 'bout how it make it look like he cain't take care of his family or some shit," my mother said.

"Yo' problem, Say, is that you wanna be the man," Uncle Lo' teased.

"Like I said, Lo', you can go fuck yourself and twice on Tuesdays," my mother said to her baby brother. And everyone on the back porch began to laugh.

The night was getting louder, closer, and hotter.

The porch was screened in and the crickets were putting

up a racket in competition with the laughter. Under the cigarette smoke there was another scent that I called "noony." My big brother said it came from some white flowers that grew in the backyard. My mother had filled mayonnaise jars with those white flowers and placed them around the porch. She said it was so that when these "sorry-ass niggas start taking off they shoes when they start playin' poker, the whole place won't stink like Fritos for a week."

As the cases of beer disappeared, the laughter and the conversation grew louder. It was impossible to understand what anyone was saying because everyone was talking at once. People slammed in and out of the screen door and the noise was like gunshots.

My uncle showed everyone how he could crush the tin Schlitz Malt Liquor cans on his forehead. My mother kept turning up the music, but everyone else kept talking louder. Some crooner on the record player kept telling everyone to "get it on." Pat danced by herself in the middle of the room. She still had on that flower sundress. But at least her wig was straightened out, I thought. My uncle's friends began to shout.

"Take it off!"

"Yeah, baby, shake it but don't break it!"

"Must be jelly 'cause jam don't shake like that!"

One guy said, "Get off the floor, Sasquatch!" And everyone laughed louder than the music.

The sun had gone down a long time ago, and I stared at the crowd through sleepy eyes. Moths flew around the back porch and up into the ceiling light. They cast strange shadows as they dived and darted, looking like tiny, dark creatures in a battlefield full of smoke, just like in one of those old war movies that Big Willie liked so much. The air was hot when you breathed it in and when you breathed it out. Lying on my uncle's chest was like being in a warm bath. He shifted me onto a different knee and I blinked awake.

A lot of people had gathered at our house. I tried to count

them, but they kept moving in and out of the back screen door. Earlier my mother had moved all four kitchen chairs onto the porch, borrowed four more from Pat, and put out the four folding chairs from the card table. She'd even put out six Carnation milk crates. Every seat was taken and more people stood along the wall, drinking, laughing, and talking. The entire neighborhood had shown up.

Pat seemed particularly happy after her husband, Gene, had gone home. Everyone called him "Gene, Gene, the drinking machine," but he usually left earlier than some of the heaviest drinkers.

Pat finally danced her almost-tall-as-the-refrigerator self over to my Uncle Lo'. She slung around her glass so much that I was afraid she'd would slosh its brown liquid right into my eyes.

"You need to put that baby down and come and dance with a real woman," Pat said. "You know I got something for you, Lo'. Somethin' I know you been missin' in those long, long months up in lockup."

With her non-drink hand, Pat lifted her flowered dress above her thigh. She was wearing white cotton panties. She swirled her middle in our faces. I could see tufts of black curly hair running down the inside of her tan thighs.

Uncle Lo' sang along with the music as he watched Pat dancing in front of us. I was going to ask him what "getting it on" meant when I looked up and saw Ainey coming at us like a runaway shopping cart.

But in one motion, Uncle Lo' shifted me from his lap with one huge hand and shoved Ainey with the other. She fell into Pat, whose drink went flying. Ainey grabbed Pat's wig on the way down, and it came off in her hand. Underneath the wig, Pat's grey braids poked out from her hairnet.

The two women started rolling around like the men did in those wrestling shows that my big brother liked. They rolled right into a table, tipping several mayonnaise jars to the floor, splashing water, glass, and "noony" everywhere.

"Fight! Fight! Fight!" my uncle's friends chanted, just like the kids at Figueroa Elementary school.

Uncle Lo' stood over Ainey and Pat, watching. He held his beer to his mouth as if it were a microphone. "This is Howard Cosell," he began, mimicking the rapid speech of the boxing broadcaster. "These two behemoths of the gridiron are going at it. You can feel the spit flying into the stands. Tonight, it's Godzilla vs. King Kong, and WHO is going to be the winner?"

Laughter boomed through the back porch. You couldn't hear the record player at all anymore. I started crawling across the floor like my baby brother did. When these fights broke out at parties, the best place in the whole house was under the table. I avoided a few still-lit cigarette butts, water puddles, and broken glass on the floor and scooted under the table, where I sat cross-legged against the back wall. I stuck my two favorite fingers back in my mouth and watched between the legs of the people standing around Ainey and Pat, who wrestled and shrieked on the floor.

Some of the people were barefoot, just as my mother had predicted. I hoped they didn't get cut on the broken glass. A few rooted for Pat, but most cheered on Ainey, and others, who couldn't make up their minds, yelled encouragement to both—which came out sounding like "Pat-Annette kick her ass."

I saw my mother head for the broom closet, where she kept her rifle, and sure enough, she came marching back across the room to point it at Ainey. Looking up into the barrel of the gun, Ainey froze like a character in a *Road Runner* cartoon.

"Say, this here ho was pushin' up on Lo' right in front of me," she complained.

"Don't care," my mother said. "I ain't gonna have you two bitches bustin' up my shit and terrorizin' my babies. You can put yo' hands down, but you gotta get the hell out of my house."

Uncle Lo' came up behind my mother and took the gun from her, grabbing the barrel with one hand and pulling her hand away from the trigger with the other.

"It's okay, Say. We didn't mean no disrespect," Uncle Lo' told her as he set the gun on one of the milk crates.

My mother looked at Ainey and Pat and said, "Party is over."

Ainey got off the floor, and Pat picked up her wig and put it back on backwards. Uncle Lo' threw an arm around each of the women and started to lead them out the back porch door.

He said, "I just bet I can think of a way you ladies can make it up to me for spoilin' my homecoming." They all seemed to be laughing at the same joke as they went down the steps together. The rest of the party-goers trailed behind them, skirting around my mother as if she were a muddy puddle of water after a drenching rain.

The next morning my mother cleaned up the back porch. She put cigarette butts and beer cans into a large tin trash can. I offered to help. I liked the clanking sound the cans made as they crashed to the bottom of the metal can. I started counting the cigarette butts as I threw them away. I was up to thirty-nine when my mother said, "Turn up that the radio, that's my song." It was Johnny Mathis singing "Chances Are."

Hauling the can into the house, I almost ran right into Big Willie, who was just coming through the front door. He was not a tall man but he was wide like a De Soto, as Uncle Lo' would say. My mother liked to say that he was "smooth, almost blue black," like a shiny new telephone. He liked to brag that the "blacker the berry, the sweeter the juice." Big Willie scooped me up and put two fingers to my lips so I wouldn't say anything. He put me down and went out to the porch. I turned up the music as loud as it would go.

Looking out the back door, I could see Big Willie walking in an exaggerated tiptoe motion toward my mother, as if he was going to scare her. But instead, he put his arms around her ample waist and began to dance with her to the music. Big Willie sang along with the tune in a voice that I thought was better than Mr. Johnny Mathis. He sang about how he grinned whenever he saw my mother.

I closed the back door so they could have some grown-folk conversation.

After that party, I found myself left with a burning question: "Who is the eighth baby that Mama had referred to?" There were only seven of us, after all. I went in search of my big sister Yvonne for answers.

I found Yvonne listening to music in her room. Yvonne, who was thirteen, had worked the entire summer babysitting for us and the neighbors to be able to afford that stereo.

"Yvonne!" I yelled in her face. Yvonne held up her hand as she bobbed to the final beat of a song. Finally, she removed the headphones.

"What, girl?" she said. "You know you don't bother me when I'm into my music."

"I got a question."

"You always got a question," she said, with resignation. "Okay, ask it before the Jacksons take me back to Indiana."

Back? We'd never been to Indiana. That was the problem with questions, I found; they always led to other questions. But I had to let that one go. I needed answers to one really important question.

"Mama said something about eight babies," I said breathless. "What's that about?"

"Damn you dumb, girl," she said. "Mama is pregnant. She think it's a baby, though it ain't even been born yet."

I wanted to ask, *You mean it's not a baby if it's not born? Then, what is it?* But I didn't ask. I just sat with my mouth open. In one of those conversations that I wasn't supposed to hear, I'd heard my mother tell Pat that the doctors had said she would die if she had another baby. I shared this knowledge with Yvonne.

"She obviously don't care," Yvonne said. "Havin' babies is just what she do."

With that, Yvonne put back on the headphones and continued bobbing to the music.

My sister Teresa arrived six months later. My mother was fine, but the doctor said she had developed high blood pressure and told her to cut down on pork and salt. She had to take a bunch of pills. My mother often missed taking her pills because she said the doctor wasn't clear whether it would hurt the baby when she breast-fed. And my mother didn't cut down on pork as far as I could see. Pork chops with gravy and rice were one of her favorite dishes. As for the salt, well, my mother seemed to believe that if you could still see food beneath the salt, you just weren't trying hard enough.

I already had two younger brothers and having a younger sister wasn't much different. I was too little to change the baby, my mother said, because I might accidently stick her with pins. But I wasn't too little to wash dirty diapers in the sink. First I had to dump the solid stuff into the toilet, then scrub the cloth on the washboard with a bar of soap until it was white again. Then I'd rinse them, wring them out, and hang them on the clothesline out back. If I did this every day, I got to rock the baby to sleep.

I would sit in the big white wooden rocker in Mama and Big Willie's room with the baby in my arms, and she would just go to sleep. It was magic. No wonder my mother liked having babies. It was with the men that my mother had the trouble.

Not much time passed before Big Willie and Mama were at it again over the color of Little Willie. I thought this particular fight had been settled with the birth of Teresa. She had the beautiful dark skin of a freshly opened Hershey's bar. Our brother Willie, however, was light-skinned and had long wavy hair, like a girl's. Big Willie made a big deal out of the fact that he and Little Willie didn't "favor."

"Black people have to go by features," he would say.

"And Little Willie's features is like some white man or some high-yellow nigga," he said. "Back in the day, they was field hands and they was house niggas. And the house niggas was a lot lighter than the field hands because the white man was up in there and raping those women and having babies by those women. Still them high-yellow niggas thought they was better than dark niggas like me. Right now, them high-yellow niggas ain't forgot that shit, and I ain't forgot that shit neither."

When this argument began, my mother would call Big Willie "color struck." I asked once what that meant and she said that Big Willie didn't trust anyone who was lighter than a paper bag.

"This here ain't my kid," Big Willie said for the hundredth time. "Look at Teresa—now that's my girl. Who you been sneakin' around with, woman?"

It didn't matter to Big Willie that my mother had taken more than one blood test to prove that Little Willie was his son.

"Features don't lie," Big Willie said.

"Look here, you ignorant-ass motherfuckah, features lie all the time," she said. "Every Black person got something mixed in them in America, including you. That's the way we is made. Sometimes them white boys was making dark-skinned babies too. Men dip they shit in any kind of hole that'll let 'em and some holes that don't."

"You seen my family. Ain't no mixin' up in there. It's like we just came out of the fields," Big Willie said proudly.

"You stupid-ass, ignorant-ass man. That boy don't just get his features from you. He gets them from me too. Did you know that my great-granddaddy was Navajo? And I got all kinds of relatives up there in Alexandria who are white."

Under her breath, my mother muttered, "Try and explain this shit to a man with an eighth-grade education."

"What you say to me?" Big Willie demanded.

"You heard me, Willie," she said. "I don't stutter."

Just then Big Willie came up behind my mother to give her one of his signature hugs but my mother turned on her heels, just as smooth as any ballerina, and drew out her .22 caliber pistol that was hidden down her blouse.

My mother kept a lot of things in her bra, including a change purse and folded dollar bills in her cleavage.

"Say, don't draw down on me," Big Willie pleaded. "You knows I don't like to fight."

It was true. Big Willie usually held my mother's arms down so she couldn't swing on him. But I had never seen him hit her.

"I'm tired of explaining the same goddamned thing to yo' ass every other week. We took mo' than one blood test *and* I told you more than once what's what. Still you don't trust what you hear. As they say, if you cain't appreciate what you got, you better go get what you can appreciate."

Big Willie hung his head and left the room. I could hear his car starting. I walked over to my mother, who had now put the gun away and sat down. I put my head in her lap and she stroked the back of my neck.

I always wondered why she couldn't just accept Big Willie's hug and wait for him to calm down, just as he had waited for her so many times. He was just trying to make up and she had overreacted. I liked Big Willie. He was one of the few stepfathers who said we could call him Pappy, if we wanted to.

Once, he took us to Knott's Berry Farm when they added rides. He said, "Why should these parks be for just the white kids." And he never made those of us who were not his natural children feel as if we were just in the way.

We took long rides in the back of his pickup out to Rancho Cucamonga to pick the oranges that grew on trees right on the traffic median. We made a game of who could gather the most, and all the way home we rode on a sea of oranges; one or two was jettisoned every time we hit a pothole. Bobby would shout, "Man overboard!" We laughed and laughed as we watched the oranges roll into traffic. Some cars behind us swerved to keep from running over the oranges. We laughed even harder.

Years later, I could not smell an orange without smiling.

Pulling into the driveway, Big Willie pretended we were in trouble for throwing oranges into traffic. But when we got in the house, he just gave us all piggyback rides.

Two

More Men in My Mother's Life

After Big Willie left, my mother started to go out at night with Ainey again. They liked to go out dancing at the Lobby Inn, a local bar a few miles from our house.

"You been playing mammy too long," Ainey told my mother. "You need to get out there and shake your groove thing!"

One of the first men my mother met after Big Willie was a guy named Monstro. That was his real name. When we didn't believe him, he showed us his driver's license. I asked him if he was named after that whale in *Pinocchio* but he said he didn't know. He wasn't big, but he was homely.

If there was a model for Mr. Potato Head, Monstro was it. He had huge eyes, a slab of meat for a nose, and ears bigger than our German Shepherd's. But even with those ears, we suspected that he was hard of hearing because he yelled all the time. A simple question like "Y'all got any salt?" came out as if through a loud speaker. Also, we suspected that there was something wrong with that big nose of his. He reeked of Hai Karate aftershave and left you coughing whenever he entered or left a room.

Monstro did not last long because he was cheap. He ate at our house almost every night but rarely took my mother out for dinner on the weekends.

Next up was Mr. Charles Driver. Bobby called him "Louie Nine Fingers," because he was missing a finger. He was generous with my mother when he had money, but he mostly just ignored us kids. My brother said Mr. Driver's finger had probably been removed to settle a debt. I just had to know so I asked him once.

"It got lost in an x-perment," he said.

"What kind of ex-peri-ment?" I pressed him, hoping for the opportunity to use the word we had learned in school that week.

"They got these guys at colleges that pays you to take drugs to see if they work, and one of them drugs had what they calls side-fex and it took off my finger."

"He was a human guinea pig," Bobby told me quietly.

"What's that?" I asked.

"Sort of a rat that doctors experiment on," Bobby whispered.

But Mr. Driver must have heard because he got up and left us. He didn't talk to me or Bobby much after that. He told my mother what Bobby had said, and she told us to apologize. We did.

Mr. Driver left soon after. I asked my mother if he had left because of us. She said no. There was an experiment somewhere, and Mr. Driver was going to try to go without sleep for two weeks.

"Crazy-ass motherfuckah only got one ball. He told me the other one got lost in some damn experiment," was the last thing my mother said about him.

A number of men followed Mr. Driver. One, whom we called Hobo Joe, looked just like this Red Devil firework cutout that showed an unshaven hobo with a cigar sticking out from between two oversized lips. In addition to filling the house with cigar smoke, Hobo Joe never bathed and smelled up the whole house with farts and toe jam. My sister Cynthia followed him around the house with a can of pine freshener.

"Don't Mess with Bill" Bill was another. He drank white lightning and cried a river every time he mentioned Maria, Mississippi—his hometown. Bill would tell us about his mama's pineapple upside-down cake, claiming that no woman could possibly cook as well as his mama. He never tired of telling everyone how wonderful life had been back home. If it had been so grand, I wanted to ask him, why had he left? I was starting to learn, however, that adults found my questions very upsetting.

Then there was a guy whose real name we never knew. Everyone simply called him Red. He was one of my uncle's friends from prison. I don't know why my mother went out with him after telling Uncle Lo' that she didn't want anything to do with his "jailbird-ass friends."

Red had been locked up for ten years for burglary and told us stories, with tears in his eyes, about a cellmate named Bad Brown. Bobby told me that Bad Brown had probably been Red's "prison wife."

"Wife?" I asked, perplexed. "I thought you said ain't no girls in prison."

"For a smart girl, you can be damn dumb," Bobby said.

Finally, I asked Red what had happened with his cellmate, and he told me that Bad Brown had got shanked one night after he'd refused to share his "keister eggs" with the rest of the cell block.

"Keister eggs are drugs smuggled into the prison in a person's butt," Bobby told me.

"Gross," I said.

Red was tall and light skinned, with a red beard and mustache that were shaved so close that they looked painted on. Unlike my mother's other boyfriends, he could cook. In fact, he cooked better than my mother.

He told us how he'd invented recipes while working in the prison kitchen, cobbling together dishes from whatever they had on hand.

"Everybody loved my food," he told us.

"Yeah, Betty Crocker with a shank," Bobby muttered.

Still, Red cooked us some of the best soul food we'd ever eaten. Just the sight of his black-eyed peas and hot water cornbread was enough to make our mouths water. We enjoyed every dish until we heard *the story*, which went something like this:

"I got me some friends that didn't contribute nothin' but they always in my pots trying to get something to eat, so I fixed them," Red said.

"What did you do?" I asked.

"My friends, they was some country-ass Bamma niggas, and they liked eatin' some possum."

"What's a possum?" I asked, through a mouth full of black-eyed peas.

"It's something that looks a little like a big rat," he said. I wrinkled my big-city nose up at that. "Anyway, one day them old country boys come 'round for some possum, and I cooked up some dog," Red said, laughing.

"Dog? Where did you get the dog?"

"It was just some stray," he replied, almost doubled over with laughter. "They liked to have killed me when they found out, but it was worth it. Them greedy motherfuckahs never came to dinner again."

"You lyin'," I said.

You weren't ever supposed to back talk an adult or call him or her a liar in my mother's house but it just slipped out. Fortunately, Red didn't seem to notice.

"Shiiiiit," he said, drawing out the word. "You put in a few good spices and a greedy motherfuckah will never know what they eatin'. I can still cook up a mess of dog when I put my mind to it."

That was it. I dropped my spoon and refused to eat anything else Red prepared. Within a few months, he was gone anyway.

We later overheard my mother telling Ainey that Red had been locked up again for burglary. It seems Red had broken into someone's house, but instead of stealing and getting the hell out of there, he stopped to fry up a steak. The people came home, found him eating in their dining room, and called the police.

After Red, my mother dated Leo. I detested Leo just about as much as I had liked Big Willie. As with all my mother's men, we gave Leo a new name—Leo the Crooked Lion. Leo oozed dishonesty, and not because he wore entirely too much jewelry for a man, or because he had two gold front teeth, but because of the way he smiled. There was something evil behind that smile, as if he was pretending to be polite while working out the best way to cut your heart out.

I walked in on Leo once, while he was shooting something in his arm. He hurled a boot at me, but I dodged it. I asked Cynthia if Leo had diabetes like our school nurse. I had seen Mrs. Silverstein injecting something into her arm, and she'd explained that the needle contained medicine to treat her diabetes.

"Naw, that idiot is a hype," Cynthia said.

I stared at her, uncomprehending.

"He is a heroin addict," she said, rolling her eyes.

I told my mother what I'd seen, but Leo denied it, telling my mother he'd caught me peeking while he was changing his pants. He'd thrown a boot at me to get me to leave, he said. I hated apologizing to Leo.

My brothers used to listen in on Leo's phone conversations, and they told me that he was turning our house into a "bookie joint"—all his calls concerned drugs or gambling.

Soon enough my mother found out for herself what he was all about.

I overheard my mother bragging to Ainey that Leo had given her a thousand dollars in cash for her birthday.

Later that evening, however, Leo came to take back part of the money.

"Man, you must be crazy, if you think you gonna come in here, give me some money, and then ask for it back like some jive-ass Indian giver," my mother told him.

"Look, Sarah," Leo protested, "it ain't just for me. It's for you and the kids. I got a line on a real good investment, and I just need part of the money back till tomorrow."

"That *investment* wouldn't happen to have four legs and be running in the Fifth at Santa Anita, would it?"

"What you talkin' 'bout, woman? I stopped playin' them ponies a long time ago."

"Then what's all them calls about?"

Leo looked as if he'd been slapped. "I thought somebody was on the other line. You ain't got no business sticking your big nose in my business."

"Yo' business and mine is the same, motherfuckah."

"I don't like no lady with no trash mouth."

"An' I don't like no sorry-ass gamblin' motherfuckah in my house."

Leo took a threatening step toward my mother with his hand raised, and the gun was drawn from her bra before he could take another step.

"Don't let the doorknob hit ya where the good Lord split ya," my mother said, waving the weapon.

Leo left, and we thought that was the end of the Crooked Lion. But he called a week later, and my mother agreed to go out with him. The night of the date, the police brought my mother home.

"If you see this man on the street, call the 77th Division," the officer said as my mother closed the front door.

We fought over the extension receiver to hear what my mother told Ainey about the night's adventures. It went something like this: She'd been waiting outside a nightclub for Leo when he walked up behind her, put a German Luger in her ear, and fished out the .22 pistol and the cash that she kept in her bra.

After Leo's exit—to wherever it was my mother's ex-boy-friends went—my mother took a break from men for a year or so. It was just as well because her kids were starting to grow up and bring home their own kinds of trouble.

THREE

Sarah's Brood

As soon as we got the phone call, we left to catch the RTD at the corner of Manchester and Broadway. We were in such a hurry that we didn't bring our sweaters and forty-five-degree morning chill set our teeth a-chattering. The phone call that had gotten us moving went something like this:

"I need to speak to the mother of Bobby Cotton."

"I'm the mama of Bobby Cotton. What's he got into?"

My mother didn't believe what she was hearing and thought the call was a prank. "If this is Terry Thomas playing some kind of joke, I'm gonna whup your ass when I see you, boy," she said.

Terry Thomas was my brother's best friend and was known as the neighborhood prankster. Maybe his parents had named him after that silly white comic with the gap in his teeth, or maybe not. Nobody seemed to know. In any case, *our* Terry thought he was hilarious. His favorite joke was to put a bucket of water over a half-open door, and then call someone from another room. After pushing the door open, you'd find yourself soaked with water. I fell for this trick once. Most of his victims were other kids like me. He wouldn't dare prank a grown-up, I thought, especially my mother.

But then my mother listened, realizing that it wasn't Terry Thomas on the line. Finally my mother said "Okay" and hung up the phone. She grabbed her mailbag-sized brown purse, took my hand in hers, and went out the door.

We headed for the nearest bus stop at Manchester and Broadway, where the number 45 bus was scheduled to stop at six a.m. We waited on the curb between two Mexicans in khaki janitorial uniforms waiting for their ride to work. We all stared down the road with the same hopeful look, as if looking for the bus would make it arrive sooner. Buses always ran ten to fifteen minutes behind in South Central. No one seemed to know why. Finally the bus arrived in a cloud of black smoke. The air brakes screamed like a dog hit by a car. Then the doors opened with a blast of heat.

We stepped into the bus. My mother deposited fifty cents. The driver looked me up and down and then stared at my mother.

"She's five," she said simply. "She rides free."

Actually, I was eight, but small for my age. I knew my mother didn't like to lie about such things but it was the end of the month, and the latest welfare check wouldn't arrive until the following week. She probably needed that extra fifty cents to pay for Bobby on the return trip, I thought.

My mother waited for me to scramble into the window seat directly behind the driver. She sat by the aisle.

"Hey, driver, do you stop near the 77th Division police station?"

The driver said nothing but pointed to the sign that said, "Do not converse with the driver."

My mother clucked her teeth, folded her arms across her ample chest, and sat back.

A man behind us said, "I'm going near there. It stops right out in front."

"Thank you," my mother said and closed her eyes.

Out the window the neighborhood passed us by—boarded-up buildings, liquor stores, pawn shops, chicken shacks, dirt lots, and gas stations. The guy behind us pulled the stopping cord directly over my head. I patted my mother's arm and pointed.

We got up and exited the bus. It was like stepping out of a hot bath into the freezer. The 77th Division police department was a tan building with a number of tall glass windows.

Just inside the door, uniformed officers crowded the front room. My mother went up to the counter, where a pretty blonde woman sat behind a desk. She was wearing a form-fitting fluffy pink sweater and matching lipstick. She looked like one of the dolls I had at home. I wanted to brush her long, straight blonde hair. Her name tag read Peg.

"How may I help you this fine morning?" Peg asked, drawing out the word *morning* like a song. Her Southern accent sounded a bit like my mother's, I thought. I wanted to ask if she was from Louisiana, too. But there was no time to discuss it. My mother got right down to business.

"I got a call and they say you got my boy down here. You might have him under the name of Robert Lee Cotton or under Bobby Cotton."

Peg flipped through some papers. "I don't see that here," she said. "Why don't you have a seat, and I'll have a look at the overnights."

We sat on a wooden bench that was covered in scratches and graffiti. I started reading some of the scrawled messages out loud.

"What's missing here? CH_ _CH." I laughed. "Put in *ur*, and that spells *church*," I told my mother. "Get it? It means *you are* missing from church." My mother nodded. "Look at this one. It says, *Fisting is for sissies*. Ma, what's fisting?"

My mother frowned, but before she could tell me to stop bothering her, Peg chimed in from across the room. "Um, you need to see Detective Conroy right away."

"Where he at?"

"He's been called," Peg said.

We waited a few more minutes before a white man in a brown suit approached us. His wide brown-and-white-striped tie was stained with red spots that might have been ketchup or blood. His brown hair and brown eyes were the same color as his suit. When he leaned over me, I could see a long brown hair coming out of his nose, and I stared at it. I wondered why no one had told him about it. It was clear that he didn't know it was there, like the flaky dandruff on the collar of his brown suit.

"You Sarah Gordon?" he asked.

"Yeah," my mother said as she stood up.

"This way," he said, pointing to a door behind Peg's desk. She gave a little wave as we passed, and I noticed her long nails were painted the same shade of pink as her lipstick.

The detective led us into a big office space divided into groups of areas, each with a sign telling what kind of police work was done there. Above one area a sign read Arson Division, and I thought maybe it had something to do with fire, because there was smoke everywhere. Maybe the whole place had something to do with fire, I thought. There was also a big cloud over Homicide Division and Bunco Squad— whatever that was. I craned my neck to see the source of the smoke, and I noticed that everyone in the room was smoking something. I counted four cigars, ten cigarettes, and a pipe.

"Can I smoke?" my mother asked.

"We would rather you didn't," the cop said. "A cigarette could be used as a weapon. Sit over there."

My mother sat in a chair on the side of a big wooden desk. I stood next to her. Nobody thought about getting me a chair.

"Look, Sarah, we got us a problem with your boy."

"Okay, what happened? And you can call me Mrs. Gordon."

She wasn't about to let him disrespect her. I thought maybe she ought to be more respectful, seeing as he was a cop. *Are you trying to get us arrested?* I wanted to ask but didn't, because I didn't want to be back-handed right in front of the detective. He didn't seem to even notice I was there.

The cop shook his head and began again.

"Mrs. Gordon," he said, clenching his teeth as though it pained him to show her any respect. "Last night your son and a boy named Terry Thomas were on top of one of the local churches with some Molotov cocktails."

"Is Bobby all right?"

"Yes, but there's a...uh...complication."

"What kind of complication?"

"He was hurt when they got him down. Terry's all right, though. Not a scratch on him."

"Yeah, okay, but what kind of scratches are we talking about on Bobby?"

"Well, he broke his arm."

My mother nodded and said, "Anything else?"

"It was a clean break, but he was in our custody at the time. The arresting officers took him to the hospital in an ambulance and then brought him back here. We're talking about some pretty serious charges here, like destruction of private property and arson."

"Did they burn down the church?"

"No, but that's only 'cause we stopped 'em."

"When can I see Bobby?"

"Soon, Mrs. Gordon," he said. "But you're going to have to sign a couple of papers first."

The detective tried to open the drawer on his wooden desk but it seemed to be stuck. Finally, he took out what looked like a butter knife and forced it open.

"Lousy fucking piece of government crap," he muttered, taking out some papers and handing them across the desk to my mother. My mother read them, and her frown deepened. She slid the papers back to the detective. "This here say that you didn't do nothin' wrong," she said.

"We didn't. We just stopped your son in the commission of a felony."

"Are the officers hurt?"

"No, but they could have been."

"Two grown men with guns facing off against two un-armed sixteen-year-old boys?"

"Yeah, but as I told you, they had an incendiary device. That means..."

"I know what *incendiary* means," my mother said. "You

ain't dealin' with your average street nigga. And I know it don't say on those papers that my boy and Terry get to go home without charges."

"Fair enough, Sarah...uh, I mean, Mrs. Gordon," he said. "We can put in there that there ain't gonna be no charges, and we can also put in there that you ain't gonna file no lawsuits." He was mocking her but it didn't matter because she had gotten her way.

"Fine," my mother said, rising to her feet. "Bring Bobby out here, and I'll sign."

Bobby was brought out of a back room. My big brother looked smaller somehow. He was bent over and his eyes were bloodshot. He was cradling his right arm, which was wrapped in a sling. It looked like he was rocking a baby. His white T-shirt was torn and his jeans were muddy. There were no laces in his sneakers.

My mother went to Bobby and tilted his chin toward her. She moved his head gently from side to side, inspecting his face with the practiced eye of a mother of eight, who regularly bandaged skinned knees and applied cool cloths to hot foreheads. When she was satisfied, she patted her son on the back and squeezed his good arm. Then she gave him that mama stare, which we all thought of as her superpower. You couldn't lie when she was giving you that stare.

"Look me in the eye, boy. Did you do what they say you did?"

Bobby nodded, his eyes cast down. He looked like he might cry.

The detective handed my mother a stack of papers and an ink pen. "Just so you know, we won't be filing charges against Terry Thomas either. His grandmother already picked him up."

My mother said nothing. She signed the papers and we left. There was no conversation on the bus ride home. Bobby and I sat on either side of my mother on the three-person handicapped bench in the front. We had the same bus and the same driver for the return trip as we'd had for the ride in. The air was still too hot.

When we got home, my mother took Bobby into her room and closed the door. I put a glass to my ear and tried to listen through the door, but I couldn't hear a thing. *Why did this always work in the movies?* I wondered. Then, I scrambled to the sofa when I saw the doorknob turn.

Bobby came out, wearing only his underwear and the sling on his arm. He went into the boys' room and closed the door. My mother called me into her bedroom. I tried to get my lie straight about eavesdropping. This was switch-whuppin' territory, and I knew it.

"Look here, gal. You ain't got no cause to talk about this to no nosey neighbors, right?" She gave me the stare. "You didn't hear nothin' at the door, right?"

"No, ma'am," I said. And I was excused.

I decided that it was best to go to the source. I went to the boys' room and gave Bobby the "shave and a haircut" knock.

The "two bits" knock sounded from the other side and I knew I could enter.

Bobby—who always seemed to be bouncing off the walls—just looked sad and tired.

"Are you okay?" I asked.

"Yeah, but Mama said not to gossip about it," he said. "I'm tired. I just want to go to sleep."

I felt bad for Bobby, and I didn't think he would get a whuppin' over the night's events. My mother probably figured he had suffered enough. I figured the same, so I left him alone.

It wasn't long before Terry Thomas came to visit, and I asked him what had happened the night Bobby had broken his arm.

"Shoot, you should've seen them motherfuckin' pigs with their guns drawn on us, like we was Dillinger or some shit," Terry said. "I ran down the ladder in the back. They got me in the alley and brought me around to the front. I looked up, and Bobby was still on the roof, looking into that police spotlight like there was pussy on the other end of it. And then the cop said on the loudspeaker, 'You can jump down or we can shoot you down.' So this crazy-ass nigga jumped onto the police car. I could see they just wanted to shoot him to shut him up. If I wasn't there as a witness, they probably would have just shot him and planted a piece on him or something. I probably saved this crazy nigga's life."

"Wow," I said. "Y'all could've been killed."

"Gonna take more than a couple of stupid cops to take me out," he said proudly, crossing his arms.

"Why was y'all trying to burn down a church?"

"We wasn't try to burn down no church. That church is the tallest thing on the block. When you up high, you can see more," Terry said. "We was gonna light them cocktails on fire and throw 'em down in the street and watch them explode, just like fireworks."

"You could have killed somebody," I said in my best mini-Mama voice.

"It was two o'clock in the morning and wasn't no cars and no people," he said. "Damn, people scared of everything nowadays."

Bobby and Terry used to take me along on some of what they called their "capers." Some of their other capers included filling barbecue pits with wood and throwing in cans of deodorant or bottles of rubbing alcohol and watching them explode. We would run behind a brick wall as Terry shouted, "Fire in the hole!" over his shoulder. But it wasn't long before my mother and Terry's grandmother caught on and punished the boys for wasting the contents of their medicine cabinets.

So Terry and Bobby found other ways of causing destruction. M-80 fireworks were readily available around the Fourth of July, and the boys never missed a chance to blow up a school toilet or some such. Their capers, however, didn't consist of just destroying bottles, cans, and toilets. I told my mother that Bobby and Terry were also accustomed to stopping on the freeway overpass on the way home from school and tossing rocks into the traffic below.

After that, Terry called me "the canary." I thought he had me mixed up with Cynthia because she was the one who liked Tweety Bird cartoons. Tweety was a canary. They should have called her the canary, I thought. But when I asked my brother why Terry kept calling me that, he said it was because "the canary" was what they called people who were snitches.

"Just remember, snitches get stitches," Bobby told me.

I stayed away from Terry and his capers after that.

Strangely, my mother didn't blame Terry for what had happened at the church, even though he was clearly the ring-leader of the stupid scheme. She still invited him over for dinner, saying something about her Christian duty to care for motherless children.

Terry lived down the street with his grandmother, brother, and sister. The mother and father were no longer in the pic-ture, for whatever reason. The grandmother was a Jehovah's Witness and she often carted the kids off to the Kingdom Hall against their will.

In the meantime, Bobby got a lot of mileage out of that broken arm. Everyone in the neighborhood signed his plas-ter cast, covering it with their crazy names—Pookie, Yum-Yum, T-Bone, Mad Dog, and others. No one except Terry seemed to have a normal name.

Terry told everyone the story of Bobby's death-defying leap from the church, until my mother ordered him not to tell it anymore.

It was just in time, too, because another neighborhood story would soon take center stage. The day before the news hit the block, my mother was out back, putting the clothes on the line, when Billy Bonner waved to her over the back fence.

FOUR

Friendly Neighborhood Spree Killer

"Boy, why you lookin' so poor-mouth?" my mother called to him over the back fence. "You young and God love you. It don't get no better than that."

"God don't love nobody but himself. I was praying to that God of yours just last night," Billy said, bringing his palms together in prayer. "I said, 'Dear Lord, give me a full house.' And it was just like he told me to go to hell, when he gave *my* full house to somebody else! And after that, I was out two hundred dollars to them Wells boys down the street. You know, the ones that live at that yellow house on the corner?"

"You don't need to be gamblin', no way. That's for folks who are tryin' to get somethin' for nothin'. If the root of gamblin' ain't greed, then my name ain't Sarah Gordon. And First Timothy 6:10 tells us that the love of money is the root of all sorts of injurious things," my mother said. "And you know God love everybody. Why don't you come on back here and get a sandwich and get some of the word of God in you before you do somethin' stupid."

"I don't think God love no sinner like me," he said.

"Billy, God knows you inside and out. Right there in Matthew 10:30, it says the very hairs of your head are counted."

Billy Bonner came to sit on the milk crates in our backyard, where my mother did most of her neighborhood visiting and Bible instruction. Billy was a very tall man, and his long legs stretched out in front of him, his black trench coat spread across the grass. His lip was swollen, I noticed, and so was his left eye. He wore a black brimless leather cap, black T-shirt, black pants, and a pair of dusty black Vans without socks.

My mother went into the house and came back with two ham sandwiches, a bag of Lays chips, and a washcloth filled with ice. She gave me one of the sandwiches and handed the other to Billy along with the washcloth. He dug into the chips, and I dug in right after him. He put the cloth to his forehead.

"I'm gonna get those Wells boys," Billy said. "They cheated in that game. I just knows they did. And then they jumped me when I told them I saw what they did."

"If you forgive those who sin against you, your heavenly Father will forgive you," my mother quoted. "That's Matthew 6:14. You should come by here for Bible study tonight."

"Cain't. I got business, but thanks for the sandwich and the company," he said. He brushed the chip dust from his fingers and the yard dust from the bottom of his coat and left through the back gate. The next time we heard about Billy, it was in the papers.

Bobby held the paper with his good hand and read aloud: "Wounds nine in spree: Gunman slays six in L.A. rampage."

"What's a rampage?" I asked.

"It's when somebody totally loses their shit and kills a bunch of people," Bobby told me and laughed. "Let me read this. 'Los Angeles, April 22, 1973. A gunman went on a one-hour shooting spree today that left at least six persons dead and nine injured, according to police. Police identified at least six shooting sites before the final shootout in which the suspect, William Bonner, was wounded and captured.

"'Bonner began his rampage when he wounded two teenagers outside a house in the Lennox area of the city, police said. After killing Otha Leavitt, fifty-three, at a house, he then took one of the victims' cars and began a series of shootings. Bonner stopped at two gas stations, two liquor stores, and two other homes—all within a one-square-mile area—shooting people with a 20-gauge shotgun, sheriff's deputy Raymond Wedmore said.'

"This shit happened down the street!" Bobby exclaimed. "And William Bonner has got to be Billy! That's that crazy nigga that's always walkin' round here dressed all in black like some kind of a ninja and shit."

"Let me see," I said, trying to grab the paper. But Bobby, at almost six feet, was much taller than I was, and he easily held the paper out of my reach.

"I'll read it," Bobby said. "You ain't gonna understand the big words, no way." He continued: "'Several of the injured were in critical condition, authorities said.'"

"Who else did he shoot?" I interrupted.

"I'm gettin' to that."

I just couldn't wait any longer. "Mama! Mama!"

My mother emerged from her room. "Girl, why you shoutin' my name like you on fire?"

"Billy shot a bunch of people around here and Bobby won't tell me who."

My mother took the paper from Bobby and read the words silently to herself. Then she swallowed and read aloud: "The gunman fatally shot an acquaintance, Raleigh Henderson, thirty-three, at a gas station, and—" My mother stopped and leaned against the wall. She read on: "'Arlene Wells, twelve, and wounded one other at another gas station; killed Smitty B. Sneed, fifty-seven, and wounded another person at Sneed's liquor store; killed Jevie D. Thompson, sixty-three, and wounded two persons at Thompson's residence, and killed his girlfriend Dianne Lore Andrea, twenty-two, at her home.

"'He was chased to another part of the city where he blocked an alley with his vehicle. He exchanged gunfire with the officers and then commandeered another car driven by Mary Felton of Inglewood...In the ensuing gun battle with police, Bonner was wounded. Mrs. Felton also suffered slight wounds in the shoulder. Bonner was taken to the USC

Medical Center Prison ward, where he was listed in satisfactory condition.'"

Arlene Wells's death hit us the hardest. Arlene—or Nina, as we had known her—was Yvonne's best friend. She was the little sister of the poker-playing Wells boys, who had supposedly jumped Billy and cheated him during their last poker party.

On the day she was shot, Nina happened to be sitting in a car at a gas station, the same station where Billy had been fired from his mechanic's job a few weeks before. He had come to the station to settle a score with his old boss. Nina just got in the way. According to the neighborhood grapevine, the whole thing probably had nothing to do with Billy's argument with the Wells boys. She had just been in the wrong place at the wrong time.

Nina's death changed Yvonne, who turned fourteen later that year. Yvonne had the best singing voice in the family, but she refused to sing a single note after her friend's death. Yvonne could draw like nobody's business, but she never drew again after Nina died. A school counselor suggested she "see somebody," but my mother told the counselor that seeing a therapist was a "white man's burden."

Yvonne had become like a stranger to us. She started sneaking out at night to meet boys, telling me that she had no intention of dying "a virgin like Nina." Yvonne bribed the rest of us with cones from the ice cream truck, so that we would keep her secrets. She had extra money, but I didn't even want to know how or from where she'd gotten it. If I didn't know, then I wouldn't have to tell my mother, I reasoned.

Yvonne was interested in one particular boy that everyone called Sugar Bear. The problem, however, was that Sugar Bear was not a boy but a twenty-year-old man. He had enlisted in the army. The neighborhood rumor was that he had a pregnant fiancée, and if he married her, he probably wouldn't get sent to Vietnam. But then the girl started claiming that the baby didn't belong to Sugar Bear, and she said she would never marry him as long as he was also dating that "fourteen-year-old whore."

So Sugar Bear's mother came to visit my mother and told her that Yvonne was putting her son's life in jeopardy by sneaking out each night to meet him. My mother hadn't known anything about Yvonne sneaking out. Yvonne denied everything, and the rest of us had been bribed into silence.

The night of my mother's confrontation with Sugar Bear's mother, Yvonne slipped out the bedroom window. When she returned, she said she had broken things off with Sugar Bear. Over the next few days, however, Sugar Bear followed Yvonne to school and asked her to come back to him. Finally, she ran home and complained to my mother.

Sugar Bear came to our front door and asked my mother if she would give her permission for Yvonne to marry him. Anyone under eighteen, he said, had to have a parent's written permission to marry.

My mother set him straight. "Man, if you don't get your crazy ass off my front porch, asking after one of my little girls, I'm gonna put some extra holes in yo' ass. Then, if you survive, I'm gonna do it again." Then my mother slammed the door in his face.

That set Sugar Bear off. He hollered about how he was going to burn down our house and everyone in it. Just in case he was serious, my mother kept a few 7UP soda bottles filled with gasoline on the back porch. She said if people started lobbing Molotov cocktail bombs at her house, she was going to throw a few back.

That summer my mother's rose bushes were dug up in the middle of the night and someone kept ringing the doorbell and running away. As the summer wore on, things seemed to quiet down. I thought perhaps Sugar Bear had been sent to Vietnam after all. But even with Sugar Bear seemingly out of the picture, we were about to face one of the most challenging times of our lives.

That summer our cousins, the Gordons, came to live with us. Considering that Ainey was tall and Uncle Lo' even taller, it wasn't surprising that their seven children had plenty of height—their youngest was nine years old and almost six feet tall. My eleven-year-old cousin, Tanya, would joke that people called her size-thirteen feet "yachts."

Conveniently for their childcare needs, Uncle Lo' and Ainey often spent staggered periods of time in jail. But that summer, both Gordon parents found themselves in jail at the same time. No one shared with me the nature of their offenses.

Our house was crowded but my mother proclaimed it her Christian duty to host our relatives. So we made cots on the floor with blankets to make room for Freddie, Ricky, Phillip, and Dana. The three other Gordon children were sent off to other relatives.

At nearly seven feet, Phillip was the tallest of the Gordon cousins. He had to duck to come through the doorway. He also had an unusually large head, for which we nicknamed him Moonie. In fact, we often referred to the Phillip's head screwdriver as the Moon-driver in his honor.

Finally, in September we were told that Ainey had been released from jail and would soon pick up her children from our house. I couldn't be there to say goodbye because it was the first day of school.

As I sat in Miss Mayfield's third-grade class, I looked out the window and saw Bobby and Phillip running across the school yard and into the building.

Miss Mayfield confronted them in the hallway. "Why aren't you boys in school?" she demanded.

Bobby didn't answer but said, "I see her," and walked over to my desk.

I didn't look up from the papers on my desk. "Just go home, boy," I told him, through clenched teeth. "Don't play one of your stupid jokes."

Phillip towered over my tiny teacher, who was probably

five feet tall at the most. In a voice that was too adult for a twelve-year-old boy, he said, "I don't go to school around here, lady, and I gotta talk to my cousin."

"And just who is your cousin?" Miss Mayfield asked.

"There she is," Phillip said, walking toward me. He stood next to Bobby, who looked as if he was going to bodily pick me up and carry me out of the classroom.

"You got to come home right now, Mary. Your house got burned down," Phillip said.

This was exactly the kind of prank that Phillip and Bobby would pull. They always liked making little kids look stupid. They seemed to think the bigger the audience, the better the joke. Glancing around the classroom, I could see that all eyes were on me.

"What happened?" I asked, looking down. "Is everybody okay?"

"It got burned down by accident," Bobby added. "Ain't nobody hurt or dead."

"Whatever," I said, and went back trying to write the perfect cursive letter *s*. They weren't going to get me with that one. It was the first day of school, and I had looked forward to it all summer. Miss Mayfield hadn't had the chance to hand out the semester's reading list yet, and that was always my favorite part.

"Okay, stay here then," Phillip said. "But you ain't got no house to go to."

"Don't be stupid, girl," Bobby said. "Let's go."

"No," I said, and I gripped the sides of my desk just in case they decided to force the issue.

Just then, Miss Mayfield intervened. "You're disrupting my lesson," Miss Mayfield said. "I'm going to have to ask you boys to leave."

"Whatever, suit yourself," Phillip said to me. Bobby gave me one last sorrowful look over his shoulder as he followed our cousin out, and for the first time I started to wonder if the house burning wasn't a joke.

A moment later, I concluded it was definitely a joke, and not a very funny one at that. But about halfway through the one-mile walk home, I just knew Phillip and Bobby had been telling the truth. I ran the last six blocks in a wild panic. I smelled it before I saw it. The blackened frame of our tiny white stucco house still stood, but the windows and doorway were black gaping holes. Our living-room couch, still giving off smoke, occupied one corner of our front yard.

Smoldering piles of wood buried what remained of my mother's recently replanted rose bush. There were wet, half-burned clumps of cotton stuffing from the sofa scattered across the ground like charred little rabbits looking for a hole. The front door had been chopped away, and all the windows were shattered. Broken glass littered the lawn, glinting in the sun like lit cigarettes.

The backyard seemed untouched. An old plaid brown sofa served as our yard furniture in one corner, the mop handle that we used to play stickball leaning against it. My mother's gardening tools had been left in a bucket, ready to be washed. Collard greens and corn stalks in the vegetable garden swayed in the wind.

Freshly laundered sheets, smelling of smoke and sunshine, hung from the clothesline. I wrapped myself in them and curled up on the backyard sofa. If I slept, I thought, we could start the day over. When I woke, it would be the first day of school again, and Bobby and Phillip would not come to my classroom with bad news. I would get the semester's reading list and discover that it included two Judy Blume books, ones I had read over the summer. There would be no burned-out house. Everything would be okay when I woke up.

I awakened to the smell of bacon and eggs. I cast off the sheets in a wild flurry. It had all been a horrible dream, and Mama was in the kitchen making breakfast. But as I shielded my eyes from the noonday sun, I saw it was not my mother but Mrs. Wells, Nina's mother, holding a plate out to me.

She had hardly left her house since her daughter had been murdered. Her sons' loud weekend parties had ceased, and the Wells house had been shut up, the curtains drawn, for months.

Mrs. Wells had lost a lot of weight. Her pink-flowered housedress hung on her tiny body like sheets on a clothesline. Her foam pink curlers stuck out from under her white headscarf.

"Hey, chile. It's just me," Mrs. Wells said, when I shrank back into the sofa. "I'm so sorry about your house."

I had not seen her since she'd brought Yvonne home after Nina's funeral. I was about to take the plate when Ainey arrived, striding across the yard.

Ainey grabbed the plate from Mrs. Wells. "Hey, thanks," Ainey said. "Ain't got no home cooking in the joint. Just got out."

Mrs. Wells looked startled. "Just bring the plate back when you are done," she said. She left through the back gate, and I could see her climb the steps of her back porch and disappear into her shut-up house.

"Scooch over," Ainey said. I obliged and she sat down next to me. "Yo' mama sent us to get you. I told her that I'd sent Bobby and Phillip to yo' school but you was too pigheaded to go with them. Everybody's at my house."

Ainey finished the breakfast, sopping up the butter with a piece of toast, and left the plate on the ground next to the sofa. Crossing the yard to her truck, she left me sitting on the couch. I picked up the plate, went out the back gate, and set the dish on Mrs. Wells's porch. Head down, I went over to Ainey's truck.

"I told you, you stupid girl," Phillip said as Bobby hoisted me into the truck. On the ride to the Gordons' house, I asked them how the fire had started.

Phillip said, "It ain't really my fault, you see. I was just mopping the floor on the back porch, and Aint Sarah had those 7UP bottles with gas in 'em. I knocked one over, and then I tried to mop it up. The mop caught fire from the hot water heater pilot, and the whole thing just blew up. We lucky we got out without gettin' kilt."

"You and Bobby was the only ones there at the time?" I asked.

The boys exchanged looks and both nodded.

"So nobody else saw what happened?" They nodded again.

I sighed and sat back, resigned to never knowing exactly how our house had met its demise.

Over the next week, we slept in makeshift beds on the Gordons' living room floor. But my mother frequently argued with her sister-in-law over money. Ainey believed my mother was due a large insurance settlement, but insurance agents claimed the fire was caused by negligence, and no money was due. We stayed another week, and then Ainey told us to leave.

FIVE

Life on the Road

I could feel the hard tile floor beneath the army-green quilted sleeping bag that I shared with my sister Cynthia. Yvonne and Morris huddled together on an overstuffed secondhand sofa, identical to the brown-and-tan plaid sofa that used to reside in our backyard.

My mother sat at a card table covered with papers. An olive-skinned man in a black outfit with a white collar sat at the other side of the table. He was a priest, the first I'd ever seen in real life.

"Mrs. Gordon, we have several Catholic charities to take the children in," the priest said.

Peeking out of the edge of the sleeping bag, I saw my mother glance over at us. I shut my eyes fast and pretended to be asleep.

"I already promised my kids that I wouldn't put them in a foster home, Mr. Martinez."

"I am a priest, and you should address me as Father Martinez," he said. "These aren't foster homes. They're good Christian families that want to help out."

But my mother wasn't buying it. "I'm not ungrateful that you let us stay here," she said, "but I want to get one thing straight. I don't call no man *Father*. The only true father is in heaven. That's Matthew 23:9."

"Mrs. Gordon, our ministry is one of a spiritual fatherhood of God's children. The Father, Son, and the Holy Spirit are one. The one God has three persons who are all equally God."

The Trinity didn't make much sense to my mother. "Jesus

Christ is God's son, and the Holy Spirit is the power that God uses or let others use to help his purpose. Jesus does not claim to be God. He calls our Father the only true God at John 17:1. And I don't think I want my kids around that Trinity nonsense. Don't you think the devil would have been busy destroying everything if God was dying on the torture stake or cross, like you people call it? When his son Jesus was killed, it was a man that was killed, not Our Lord the Father. Yes, Christ was the greatest man that ever lived, but he was a *m-a-n*," she said, spelling it out as if the priest were an ignorant child. "Christ and God is not the same thing."

I had been up all night listening to my mother and the priest arguing back and forth in hushed voices. It seemed to me that my mother would make a Jehovah's Witness out of this priest, if we were allowed to stay just a few more days. But it was not to be.

The priest sighed heavily and said, "Mrs. Gordon, I've already let you stay here for a week, longer than any other family we've helped recently, even good Catholic families, because I knew you had trouble, but I can see now that this is hopeless. We have to make room for other Christian families in trouble. I can give you a phone number of someone I know at the Red Cross, and maybe they can find a stable situation for you."

The priest had given up. There would be no "good Christian homes" for us. Still, I wondered what these homes were like. Did crucifixes hang on the walls? Did statues of saints cover every surface? That was something my mother definitely wouldn't like. I could imagine her scorn for "bowing down to graven images."

"I hope one day that you find the true God because you have a good heart," she told the priest as she rose to her feet.

The priest clearly didn't know that his "false religion" was an instrument of Satan, she told us later. He was just a victim like a lot of people in this world. We shouldn't blame him, she said. We should pray for him.

In my mother's mind, she was trying to help the priest and not the other way around.

I didn't see the expression on the priest's face because I was still pretending to sleep, but I'll bet it was one of surprise. My mother thanked the priest and walked over to us. I held my breath.

"Girl, you supposed to be pretending to sleep, not dead," my mother told me. "Y'all get up. We're going to your uncle John's tonight."

I nudged Cynthia awake, and she threw back the sleeping bag. After three weeks on the road, we were getting used to being asked to leave at the oddest hours.

We rummaged through our shopping bags, pulling out sweaters and scarves. It was very early still and forty-five degrees outside, according to a thermometer in the church garden.

The church on Figueroa Street was located near a bus stop. We knew all the bus stops in the neighborhood, because we had been doing a lot of our sleeping on buses and benches. Some drivers were understanding and let us make the round trip without paying again, but most just told us to get off at the end of the line. We usually walked across the street and caught the same bus on the return trip. Of course, we had to pay again. It was cheaper than a motel, my mother explained.

On these rides, Yvonne kept us younger kids occupied by playing hand games with us, so that my mother could sleep. Our singing almost drowned out my mother's snoring. We would play hot hands, which consisted of putting your hands, palms down, on another person's hands, and quickly jerking them away before they slapped the back of your hands. If they got you, then it was your turn to slap their hands, and so forth.

Or we would play "My sailor went to sea, sea, sea." The song went something like this: "My sailor went to sea, sea, sea. To see what he could see, see, see. But all that he could see, see, see was the bottom of the ocean. See, see, see." The other passengers seemed to get a kick out of it. Only once did a driver tell us to keep it down.

Morris, who was six, said that hand games were for girls, and he curled up alongside my mother and went to sleep. I felt particularly sorry for Morris. Uncle Sam had refused to take him in along with my brothers Bobby and Steven. Small children were like girls, he said, "incomprehensible, and they cried too much." Meanwhile, Big Willie's parents had taken in four-year-old Willie and two-year-old Teresa.

During the bus ride to my mother's older brother's house, Yvonne grew very quiet. We couldn't get her interested in our usual hand games. She hated Uncle John. Yvonne told us once that it was because Uncle John had tried to touch her when she was twelve. No one believed her. Yvonne always seemed to be imagining that someone was trying to touch her. She even claimed that Big Willie had tried to do so, when he carried her to bed one night after she had fallen sleep on the sofa. We didn't believe that either.

Yet we knew that Uncle John often chased young girls, usually white girls. My mother said he picked up "strays" at the Hollywood bus station. She said they all thought they were coming to L.A. to be big stars, but they just wound up selling their "coochie-pop" on Sunset Boulevard.

My uncle John lived in a studio apartment in the West Adams district, near the University of Southern California. His apartment was on the fourth floor, and there was no elevator. We slogged up the steps carrying the shopping bags of everything we owned. At the door we heard the soft hum of a television set from inside. A Cal Worthington commercial was blaring that everyone should "Go see Cal. Go see Cal," and if he couldn't make a deal on a used car, he would "eat a bug." My mother knocked and knocked, but no one answered. We walked back downstairs and waited in the lobby. Luckily, there was no security in the building, and a nice bench. We slept.

The next morning, as I was waking up, I saw my uncle

John tiptoeing past us. He was halfway out the door to the street when I shouted, "Uncle John!" He quickly closed the door and turned to us.

"Hey, kid," he said. "I was just getting home."

My mother rubbed her eyes and said, "Looked to me like you was sneaking out."

"No, Sarah, I just got back. Come on up."

He turned around and led us up the stairs. I counted sixty in all.

His studio apartment was sparsely furnished but still managed to look a mess. Books and papers littered the floor, and clothing was strewn about, even flung over the lampshade. A sleeper sofa took up most of the space, and we could see a body-shaped lump under the ratty blue woolen blanket.

"Hey, get up," my uncle said, shaking the bed. "We got company."

Emerging from beneath the covers was a girl of about sixteen. She had long blonde hair and a bad case of acne that seemed to extend from her face to her shoulders. She let the cover slip and we saw her small breasts, like two strawberry cupcakes.

"Here, cover up," Uncle John said, and tossed her a T-shirt that said "burn, baby, burn" on it. When I asked Uncle John what that meant, he said that was what people had shouted during the Watts Rebellion of 1965 as they burned buildings. Some people shot at the fire trucks, he told me, to keep them from putting out the flames.

"You can only push people so far," Uncle John said, "before you leave them with destruction as the only way to express their anger against the white man's system."

He had not participated in the rebellion, he said, but he had been with the protesters in spirit.

"John, why you filling that girl's head with all this Black versus white stuff?" the blonde girl asked. "Why don't you tell her that some people call it a riot and not a rebellion?"

"What the hell you know about it? You was just in the

third grade when it all came down," Uncle John said. My mother rolled her eyes and sat on the edge of the bed. She lit a cigarette. We put down our shopping bags and sat on the floor.

"John don't allow no smoking in his place," the girl said. My mother just sighed and rolled her eyes again. "You know that's bad for you," the girl added.

"So is sleeping with a man old enough to be your pappy," my mother replied.

The girl scrambled out of bed, grabbed her dirty, fringe suede bag, and stalked into the bathroom. She wasn't wearing anything under the T-shirt, I noticed.

Uncle John said, "Look, Say, I gotta go to work. We gonna work this out later. Try to be polite at least. She's a real nice girl."

He knocked on the bathroom door. The girl giggled and then said, "Come on in, pappy." Uncle John went into the bathroom. I don't know what was said or done inside, but shortly after, Uncle John came out, grabbed his hat, and left.

Yvonne searched the cabinets above the hot plate, looking for food, while my mother turned her attention to the black-and-white TV.

When the girl came out of the bathroom, she was dressed in a red halter top, white shorts, and blue platform open-toed shoes that increased her height by five inches.

My mother stared at the TV. I don't know what she was looking at. The horizontal was broken, so the set was just showing squiggly lines. We could hear the Tarn-X commercial entreating everyone to stop using elbow grease to clean their silver. "You don't want to go on, rubbing and scrubbing until your hands are raw," the commercial advised.

I spoke up: "What's your name?"

"I'm Melanie," she said.

"A silly white name for a silly white girl," my mother said.

It was the girl's turn to roll her eyes, but she made an effort to be polite.

"Your brother told me all about you. Can't we be friends?" Melanie asked, extending her hand. "I'm sorry about what happened to your house."

My mother leaned past the girl's outstretched hand, and turned the TV up even louder. Melanie, pretending she hadn't noticed the snub, walked over to Morris and me.

"Do you sell coochie-pop?" Morris asked her.

"What?"

I jabbed him in the ribs, but he kept on. "My brother Bobby say that all of Uncle John's girls sell coochie-pop."

I whispered in his ear, "That ain't nothing real, just shut up."

I pinched Morris on his arm, and he squealed. "Ma, Mary pinched me."

"Stop it," my mother said, her attention still fixed on the squiggly lines.

"Do you want to see my coochie-pop?" Melanie asked Morris.

That got my mother's attention. "Don't be showin' your honky ass to my kids," she said sharply, without turning around.

That was the last straw. Melanie gathered her bag and left, slamming the door behind her.

Yvonne brought us bowls of creamed corn and rice. It was all she could find in the cabinets, she said. We ate, and then we slept in front of the flickering TV.

My uncle John came back to his apartment at six that evening. The first thing that he wanted to know was what had happened to Melanie.

"She gone and good riddance," my mother said. "John, what the hell do you think you doin' with that little honky bitch? She way under age. You want to get put *under* the jail?"

"Look, Sarah, my landlord ain't gonna let all these kids stay here. This is an adults-only kind of place," he said. "Y'all can stay the night but then you got to find some other place to go."

Without another word my mother started picking up shopping bags and hustling us out the door. We caught the bus to the Cameo Theater in downtown Los Angeles. For one dollar for adults and fifty cents for children, we could stay through the quadruple feature, which included *The Doberman Gang*, *Fists of Fury*, *Five Fingers of Death*, and *Cotton Comes to Harlem*.

We really liked *The Doberman Gang*, about a pack of dogs that are taught to rob a bank. "See six savage Dobbies taught to bite the long arm of the law!" the trailer proclaimed.

By our third viewing of the movie, *The Doberman Gang*, we had memorized the words to the theme song. We burst out laughing as we finished. That's when we saw the guy with the flashlight.

"Y'all cain't stay here," a voice said beyond the light.

"Why not? We paid," my mother said, covering her eyes as she blinked into the light.

"Y'all paid for one round, but y'all been here all night," said the voice as he clicked off the light. Through the flicker of the movie screen we could see a tall, dark-skinned boy of about seventeen.

"Look, if it was up to me, y'all could stay, but the manager told me to come down here and say you got to go."

"Let us stay just until this one movie is over. The kids sure do like it. Okay?" my mother asked.

"I'm gonna get fired," he said. "Look, this is what y'all do. The manager leaves at ten at night. Y'all come back then and I'll let you in the back."

My mother had already started to gather our shopping bags. She was never particularly good at asking favors from anyone.

We walked out onto Broadway. It was about five p.m., and traffic downtown was at its usual rush hour standstill. People passed us, and a few stared at this large woman with her four ragged charges, each carrying a shopping bag. But mostly we went unnoticed. My mother began to discuss foster homes.

My mother turned to me, Cynthia, and Morris, and said, "Me and Yvonne can do this, but I cain't put y'all through no more. We gonna take the bus to the welfare office and see about foster homes."

I stumbled backwards as if I'd been hit. *Weren't foster homes for poor kids with no parents?* I thought. *Didn't they molest kids in those places? Didn't they kill kids in those places?* "We'll be good, Mama," I pleaded. "We ain't gonna be singin' in the movies no more."

"It ain't y'all," my mother said. "It's just that these streets don't have no pity for my babies."

"We ain't no babies," Cynthia screamed, and threw herself on the sidewalk, exactly like a baby. I joined her and I pulled Morris down next to me. We did our fair share of kicking and screaming.

People started to gather as we screamed, kicked, and cried right in the middle of the sidewalk.

"Okay, okay," my mother relented. "I ain't gonna put y'all in no foster care."

We stopped crying immediately and followed my mother to the downtown L.A. Greyhound bus terminal. We sat in the very uncomfortable plastic chairs. After we had checked all the phone booths and paper machines for stray coins, we came up with fifty cents. Attached to each chair was a coin-operated small black-and-white television. You could watch ten minutes for a dime. Cynthia, Morris and I crowded around one chair and watched an entire episode of *Green Acres* for thirty cents. We were careful not to sing the theme songs too loudly, although it was hard when Eva Gabor threw open the doors of her house, and told everyone how much she just adored a penthouse view. "Darling, I love you but give me Park Avenue."

The next day we *did* go to the welfare office. But as luck would have it, they had found us an apartment on Ninety-Second and Avalon. It wasn't furnished, but we didn't care. We spread our clothes out on the floor like cots and retrieved a few milk crates from the alley for furniture. Morris and I found a few cinderblocks and a board that had been discarded from a construction site next to the apartment building, and we had a dining room table.

My mother promised to scour the Salvation Army Thrift Store for regular furniture as soon as she received her first cash welfare payment. We didn't care that it was one bedroom, we were just glad to have a roof over our heads. Soon we were all together again. My mother retrieved Steven and Bobby from Uncle Sam, and Big Willie's stepmother dropped Teresa and Willie off at our new place. We were a whole family again.

Our weeks of homelessness had forced my mother to give up her job as a nurse's assistant at a convalescent hospital. The emergency assistance from welfare would help us, she said, while she looked for work. We were given a voucher for food stamps. My mother had the lights and gas turned on with credit. We had shelter, food, gas, and lights—more than we had had the previous month.

The first few weeks at the Avalon Apartments passed without incident. But then one morning, we were woken by a tremendous crash in our bathroom. Right atop our toilet was the shattered remains of the upstairs neighbor's toilet. It was a blessing that nobody had been using either one at the time of the accident, my mother said.

My mother called the landlord from the phone booth on the corner of Ninety-Second Street—we didn't yet have our own phone—and came back looking angry.

"Stupid slumlord said he ain't gonna get nobody over here for a week," my mother told us. "Y'all will have to use the corner Texaco bathroom or the alley. Take yourself a ho-bath before you go to school."

"A ho bath," Yvonne explained, was where you wiped your cooch, pits, and backside in the sink with a washcloth.

It was inconvenient to go the bathroom at the Texaco and dangerous to go in the alley, where the neighborhood winos would throw rocks if you tried to pee in their territory. Now, too, we could hear everything that transpired in the floor above us, which was how we found out about Miss Mai and her girls.

"This ain't no hotel!" Miss Mai would yell at her customers. "So what if there ain't no bathroom! You here to buy pussy, not to take a shit!"

We'd initially thought the girls going in and out of the apartment were her daughters. We were partly right. Miss Mai had five teenage girls—four of whom were her daughters—and three other women in the apartment. They were all what my brother called "working girls."

We had decided to live and let live, seeing as we had little choice in the matter. But Miss Mai's household and ours were on a collision course. It all began one afternoon as we were walking home from school. Miss Mai met Yvonne, Cynthia, and me outside our apartment.

"Hey, girl, why don't you come around sometime," Miss Mai said. "You got yourself a nice rack. We could make a lot of money together."

Yvonne grabbed Cynthia's hand and mine and propelled us into our apartment. My mother said she would have a talk with the neighbor the next time she saw her.

Miss Mai was short, wide, and very fair skinned. When she was younger, she could pass for white, some said. She'd once had long, stringy red hair but had lost most of it due to alopecia. To hide her condition Miss Mai wore wigs and turbans, and painted-on eyebrows.

In her customary satin red men's pajamas, she looked like a jigsaw puzzle that had been put together from several different boxes. With her white turban, she looked like Santa Claus, Bobby said.

Soon after the incident on the street, my mother confronted Miss Mai.

It was one of those hot summer nights when almost everyone seemed to be hanging over the rails outside their apartments. A few front doors were open and the TVs were all blaring the same episode of *Sanford and Son*. The courtyard lights had never worked, but the streetlamp just outside the apartment's entrance illuminated the courtyard. When Miss Mai came through the rusty metal front gate, my mother stepped into the light and started laying down the law.

"You keep your filthy mouth to yourself," my mother said.

"This filthy mouth is worth a lot of money," Miss Mai said and licked her full lips. "Welfare don't pay for my lights and gas."

"Stay in your pea patch, bitch," my mother said. "And me and mine will stay in ours."

"You can try to kick my ass, but you cain't," Miss Mai said.

Then, right there in the courtyard, Miss Mai turned and pulled down her red satin britches to extend her large pale rear toward my mother. And just as my mother drew her foot back to land a blow, Miss Mai pulled up her pants and hopped out of the way in one fluid movement.

"Why you pullin' up your pants?" a voice called from a balcony above. "We done all seen it." And everyone began to laugh.

Miss Mai blushed and walked toward my mother. "I mooned you and you was gonna kick me. You crazy bitch," she said.

"I'm gonna do more than that if you don't stay away from my door," my mother said, reaching into her purse. I guessed she was going for her knife, since she had pawned all the guns that had survived the fire. She took a step toward Miss Mai, who promptly bolted up the stairs. We could hear her sliding the locks on her apartment door as if she were a jailer locking a cell door against a dangerous inmate.

"Ain't exactly Ali versus Frazier," a voice called from the balcony crowd.

The spectators laughed as they went back into their apartments.

We tried to stay away from Miss Mai and her girls. One

day, however, Cynthia, Morris, and I were walking past the construction site where Miss Mai's girls were collecting rocks. They started to chase us, throwing stones. They didn't hit us, but we were scared witless and ran all the way to school.

We didn't tell our mother. Instead, after my mother had left to look for work, we climbed out the bathroom window and went to school by way of the alley.

A few weeks later Cynthia came tearing into the apartment. She grabbed a six-pack of empty RC cola bottles that I had spent all weekend collecting—they were worth sixty cents in returns, and I had already figured out what I was going to buy with it.

"What you doin' with my bottles, girl?" I demanded.

"One of them nasty men at Miss Mai's house touched me, and I'm gonna get him."

Before I could say a word, Cynthia was out the door. I was halfway across the courtyard when I saw her tossing one of the bottles at some guy. Laughing, he caught the unbroken bottle as if it were a game of slow-pitch softball.

Looking at the other five bottles in her six-pack, he said, "You better stop befo' you get yourself in trouble."

But Cynthia was beyond listening to anything he had to say. Furious, she broke another bottle on the curb and pitched the jagged glass at him. He reached up to stop it, catching the jagged end and cutting his hand. Cynthia grabbed another bottle and hurled it at his head. The pitch went wild, and the glass shattered on the brick wall behind him, sounding like a gunshot. Cynthia cracked the rest of the bottles on the sidewalk and pitched the jagged ends at him, like a baseball pitching machine. Throwing up his hands, the man tried to ward off the broken bottles, some striking him in the chest. He had long since stopped laughing, and shards of glass covered the courtyard.

Of my mother's daughters, Cynthia was the smallest and the fiercest. People sometimes called her Skinny Minnie after a roller-derby queen who skated for the L.A. Thunderbirds.

At four foot nine and ninety pounds, people often underestimated Cynthia's strength. She sometimes lifted weights with the neighborhood boys, and she could dead-lift more than her body weight. I had twenty pounds on her, but she could lift me up and slam me onto the floor when we had fights.

As I stood next to her in the courtyard, I could feel the rage shuddering through her small frame. All was quiet except for Cynthia's rapid breath and the guy's sobs. He curled over his injury, squatting in the courtyard like a dog trying to push out his business.

Then, as if suddenly shaken awake, the guy rose to his feet, yelling, "Fucking bitch, you cut me!"

He's going to rush us, I thought. *Could we both take him?*

But he didn't try to rush us. He was hurt. I was torn between trying to help him and letting him bleed to death. He had tried to molest my sister, after all. Then, I realized, he wasn't a man at all, but a boy of no more than thirteen years old. He wore the typical teenage uniform of a T-shirt and Levi's with the too-long cuffs rolled up at his ankles. Rail thin, he probably weighed no more than Cynthia, with pimples across his nose and cheeks and braces on his teeth. He was just a kid—why hadn't I noticed that before?

Before I could decide what to do, Miss Mai in her satin pajamas came barreling down the stairs two at a time. "What you little heffas den done to my boy?"

She took off her red satin top and started wrapping the boy's hand with it. Her upper half was naked, and I was momentarily transfixed by her breasts, which resembled two ashy eels. "I'm gonna kill you little heffas," she said. "You ain't gonna get away with maimin' my baby."

"*Your* baby?" I asked. Now I was the one shaken awake. Without wanting to hear her answer, I grabbed Cynthia and went into our apartment. We sat in the bedroom closet, in the dark with our backs against the wall. Although we'd covered our ears, we could still hear the sirens of the fire department paramedics as they arrived.

We were fortunate that the rest of our siblings were still at school and Teresa and Willie were at their grandmother's house. But it was unlucky, too, because we were the only ones at home. We were still sitting in the closet, covering our ears, when my mother came home.

"Where y'all at?"

We looked at the whites of each other's eyes in the dark and scrambled out in a rush to get to my mother first. It all came out in a rush.

"This guy, who was Miss Mai's baby, felt under Cynthia's shirt, and she threw my RC cola bottles at him. There was so much blood. They called the police. Are we gonna get put in jail?"

My mother looked at the two of us, both speaking at once. Her eyebrows went up, and she smiled that beautiful grin that always revealed a little tobacco stuck on her bottom lip.

"Y'all calm down," she said. "I came to get you because we got us a house and I got a new job." We both ran to our mother and hugged her around the middle. Then we released her just as quickly because such displays always embarrassed her. "Now, y'all always remember this in case you forget that your Heavenly Father answers prayers."

My mother had reassembled her brood before Miss Mai, her girls, or her "baby" could get home from the hospital. We intended to move from the Avalon Apartments that same afternoon.

We had no furniture to speak of, and we left behind our homemade table, along with a few crates. We shoved our stuff back in shopping bags and caught the RTD bus across town to our new home on 113th Street in South Central Los Angeles.

The driver gave us a funny look. But my mother paid for herself and all eight of her children, including those under five, so he didn't say too much about all the extra bags.

As we climbed the stone steps to our new house, we marched into it with the pride of new owners rather than new renters. The grass in the front yard was almost as tall as me, and through the green stalks I could see a sign that read, *Adults Only*.

I pulled on my mother's shirt, and pointed to the sign.

"You are the world's most worried-ass child," my mother said. "Don't worry, we worked something out."

I exhaled. I was hoping the sign was wrong because the last thing I wanted in the world was to return to Avalon Apartments with Miss Mai and her girls.

There were no apartment buildings anywhere on our new street, and I was glad of it. The houses all had porches, so there was always somewhere to play on rainy days, and somewhere cool to go when it was hot inside. The house smelled of fresh paint. My mother told us to open all the windows, and she left the front door open. Plenty of kids lived on our street, although my mother approached any new friendships with caution.

"I don't see why y'all have to hang out with these here kids," she said. "Y'all got all the friends and enemies you need right here in this house."

Still, my mother herself found a new friend in Bill, who lived directly across the street from us with his wheelchair-bound mother. Bill was a master mechanic. He could fix almost any car when he wasn't drunk. The trouble was that Bill was drunk most of the time.

Bill, Ainey, and my mother started hanging out together. The group was complete when Uncle Lo' and Uncle John visited. Everyone thought I was strange because I liked to hear their grown-up stories.

My mother bought a house full of secondhand furniture, so there was somewhere for everyone to sit. I would settle onto the lap of one of my uncles, waiting for the stories to begin. It didn't matter which uncle as long as he kept my mother from throwing me out of the room.

"Y'all remember that old stringy-haired white bitch that lived on the corner when we was kids?" Uncle Lo' asked.

"You mean the one with the mole in the middle of her foe-head?" Uncle John said.

"None other," Uncle Lo' continued. "We used to call her a witch."

I wanted to ask if she really had been a witch, but I knew this would call unwanted attention to myself. Besides, the story was being told *over* me and not *to* me. Best for the grown-ups to forget I was there.

"She wasn't no witch, Lo'," my mother said. "She was just an evil old cracker."

"Why was she evil, Say?" Bill asked.

Ainey just smiled. I had the impression that she had heard this story before.

"That bitch was evil because she taught her parrot to call us niggas when we was on our way to school."

"Niggas on da way ta school! Niggas on da way ta school!" Uncle Lo squawked, in his best parrot voice.

"Yeah, yeah," my mother said. "And one day, John picks up a big rock and knocks that fucking bird right out of his cage."

Everyone started to laugh as Uncle Lo' flapped around the room, his big arms outstretched like wings. "Niggas on da way ta school! Niggas on da way ta school!" he squawked. "Rawk! Rawk!"

"I think ya musta kilt that bird because we didn't see it after that."

More and louder laughter followed.

"Yeah, but it wasn't so funny when Mama found out. Right, John?"

"Yeah, our mama took in washin' for that old witch, and she got fired. Mama near 'bout beat the flesh off my yellow ass."

They all laughed some more.

Uncle Lo' said, "We couldn't walk nowhere to get to the colored school 'cept past that old bitch's house. You caused so much trouble, John."

The grown-ups all laughed heartily until my mother said, "You know what, John? You just might be responsible for us all ending up here in California. That old white bitch told all the other white folks in the neighborhood what had happened, and then they wouldn't give Mama no more wash work," she said. "Then Daddy left, and we had to move to Seattle so Mama could get that job in the tuna-canning factory. When the factory closed we all came out here."

"Well, it sure was worth it," Uncle John said.

"Where was Aint Dorothy?" I asked, and everyone went silent.

"Girl, get out and go play with the other kids," my mother said. "Damn girl, always up in grown folks' conversation."

I looked up at my uncle for support, but he shook his head. I climbed off his lap and left the room. Sitting on the porch, I knew I shouldn't have mentioned Aint Dorothy.

Aint Dorothy was my mother's older sister. I used to sit on her lap in the back seat of our car, and she would make *wheeee* sounds whenever we went downhill. Then she would lift me off her lap and tickle me. She would always ask, "Am I your favorite aunt?" and I would reply, "Yes, you're my only aunt."

She found my response particularly funny, and it became our standard greeting every time I saw her.

Aint Dorothy, I found out, had died of pneumonia after one of her "Houdini disappearances" from a mental hospital. The adults always whispered when they spoke of her.

Still, by listening in to grown folks' conversations, I had learned that the last time Aint Dorothy escaped from the "banana factory," it had been during a rainstorm. When she was found, she had a temperature of 103.

Several weeks later, they sent my mother Dorothy's belongings—an empty lipstick tube, a torn wallet, and a bundle of clothing—along with a note that said Aint Dorothy had been buried in a numbered plot. They'd had to bury her, the note said, because it had taken too long to find a relative.

Once I overheard my mother telling Uncle John on the phone that she had tried to get Aint Dorothy to stay at our house, but my aunt had opened all the windows and doors at two a.m., saying aliens were coming to take everyone away. I felt sad that they had sent us her clothes. *What had they buried her in?* I wondered.

I went down the street to play kickball with some of my friends, but I was thinking about Aint Dorothy. When everyone had gone to bed, I found my mother sitting at the table, smoking a cigarette and reading the newspaper. I stood in the doorway, waiting to be noticed.

"What you doing up, girl? You know you gotta get up for school tomorrow."

Sliding into one of the chairs across from her, I asked, "Ma, what happened to Aint Dorothy on the day that Uncle John killed that bird?"

"So that's what's keeping you up," she said, and I thought I saw her smile. "Dorothy refused to go to school that day because our daddy hadn't come home for days," she said. "Dorothy said somebody needed to be home in case he showed up."

"Did he?"

"Yeah, he always dragged his sorry ass home sooner or later after tomcatting around."

I wanted to ask my mother more questions about her father, since she had never spoken of him before. I thought that grandfathers were supposed to be like Heidi's in the Shirley Temple movie—kindly old men who would rescue you from gypsies and take you to their farms to live. I knew, too, that if I asked more questions about him, I would risk being sent to bed without any answers at all. The safest bet was to stay on Aint Dorothy.

"Ma, what happened to Aint Dorothy's clothes?"

"I took 'em to Goodwill," she said, and turned her attention back to the paper. "Now, go to bed."

I dreamed of Aint Dorothy and long car rides that night,

and I could still hear her *wheeee* whenever we sped downhill.

After Aint Dorothy left our lives, Butch Doss came to occupy a place in it. He lived next door with several brothers and sisters. No one ever spoke of a father. His mother, Peggy Doss, drove a royal blue Batman-style Cadillac.

Mrs. Doss was a big churchgoer, and she had so many hats that my brother Bobby just called her the Mad Hatter. My mother said Mrs. Doss's church was one of those places where people "jumped up and down, testified, and did the Hully Gully dance, while pretending they were talking in tongues." My mother referred to it as "one of them pagan-ass churches."

The Doss house was within ten feet of our home and gospel music blared from every window and door at all hours. Butch Doss spent most of his weekends at our house, avoiding his mother and her church. Yvonne and Butch used to hang out in the girls' room—one shared by Yvonne, Cynthia, and me. Teresa, still small, slept with my mother. The house rule was that the door had to stay open, and a third person needed to be in the room with Yvonne and Butch.

One summer day, racing into our room to grab the kickball, I ran right into a locked door. I banged on it and shouted. Finally, Yvonne poked her head out.

"What the hell you want, girl?"

"I want my ball."

"Ain't no ball in here."

"Yeah, it is. I can see it right there under the bed."

I pushed passed Yvonne and found Butch sitting on the bed in his underwear. Getting the kickball was now the last thing on my mind.

"Ooooo, I'ma tell Mama," I said, and ran off before either of them could grab me.

My mother came into the room and suddenly they were all innocent—fully clothed, sitting on the floor, and pretending to read the Bible. My mother didn't miss a beat. "Butch been spendin' too much time over here," she said.

And right then and there, Butch asked my mother if he could marry my fourteen-year-old sister.

"Hell no, boy," my mama said. "You ain't nothin' but no chile yourself. You ain't fully cooked yet. And she'll never blame me when you start cheatin' or beatin' on her because you don't know no other way. If you really want to marry her, you can do that in a few years, and she can say yes or no on her own."

Unhappy with my mother's decision, Yvonne didn't speak to her for a week. She developed a fascination with phone books and dialed a lot of numbers each day while my mother was at work.

"Who you callin'?" I asked her.

"None of your beeswax," she said. "You stupid canary. You always gotta be up in somebody else's business."

Bobby came into the room singing. "Yvonne and Butch, sitting in a tree, k-i-s-s-i-n-g," Bobby sang, making smacking noises. "She's tryin' to find her good-for-nothin' father, so he can let her marry that sorry-ass dude next door."

Yvonne glared at me as she held the phone to her ear, waiting to connect with someone on the other end. Finally, Yvonne said into the receiver, "Are you Roy Randolph?" He must have said yes, because she went on to say, "So, do you know a woman named Sarah Gordon, who went to Compton College a long time ago?" He must have replied yes again, because she said, "Then I'm your daughter, Yvonne."

She listened awhile and then said, "Yeah, Steven is here, too. Yeah, he's the same."

Steven was our oldest brother. He had developmental delays, but we were all under strict instructions to call him "slow." He was the tallest of the boys at over six feet, and, at two hundred pounds, the heaviest. He weighed himself every day on the bathroom scale because he wanted to grow up to be a professional wrestler like Victor Rivera, his hero. Steven had read somewhere that weight was important for a wrestler.

Steven had many habits that we were expected to ignore, like bumping his feet on the sides of any doorway that he entered. At other times, he would pull straw from the broom, twist them into shapes that resembled people, and pretend they were tiny wrestlers. During his imagined epic battles, he would pretend to be a wrestling announcer with a running commentary while he crashed his straw wrestlers into one another. The backyard always looked like a farmyard, where bales of hay had exploded. My mother didn't seem to mind buying a new broom every week.

"He likes it and it ain't hurtin' nobody," she said.

Whenever anyone met Steven, they never knew he was "slow" because he had an incredible memory. He could recall almost anything he had ever read. You would have to talk with Steven for hours before you began to realize that he didn't understand much of what he read. At one point, he read everything he could about Adolph Hitler, and somewhere he got hold of pro-Nazi literature and kept referring to Hitler as a "good, kind, and brilliant leader." It was no good us telling him that was not how history books described Hitler. Steven had read it somewhere, so it had to be so.

Sometimes the neighborhood kids would chase Steven home, throwing rocks at him and calling him "retard." Once, Steven turned on the kids, took one boy, lifted him over his head, and slammed him to the ground. Steven was sent to the "special kids' school" after that. On Monday through Friday, the short bus stopped at our house and took him to special classes at Locke High School.

Steven and Yvonne had a father in common—Roy Randolph. My mother had been with him for five years after college, but he had disappeared from her life for ten years after that—that is, until Yvonne found his phone number in the white pages.

Later that day, Roy Randolph drove to our house in his black Chevy Impala. He sat in his car near the curb with the engine running, as if he were preparing for a quick getaway after a bank robbery.

My mother, arriving home from work in her white nurse's uniform, did a double take at the car parked at the curb. A tall man, who bore a striking resemblance to Steven—wide of girth and six feet tall—stepped out of the car.

"What you want, Roy?" my mama said, as if she'd last seen him the day before.

"I wanna see my kids," he said.

"Then come on in and see 'em," she said.

Roy Randolph visited for the entire day. He tried to question Steven but got very few answers. He asked how he and Yvonne were doing in school. Steven shrugged. Yvonne ditched school most days and could barely read, but she lied to her father about her success.

"If you graduate with honors, I will buy you a car," he told her. "I promise." He crossed his heart and held up a Boy Scout salute when he said this, which I thought was rather dumb.

My mother sucked her teeth and looked away.

"What's that on your boots?" I asked, noticing that his work boots were covered in white dust.

"I'm in construction," he said. "I built most of those big buildings going up downtown."

He made it sound as if he'd done it all by himself.

Roy Randolph had a well-trimmed mustache and a goatee that he kept stroking like a favorite pet. His full upper lip was twice the size of his bottom one. Bobby said Roy Randolph's lips were "serious soup coolers." He wore jeans and a blue dress shirt with the sleeves rolled up to reveal muscular, veiny arms.

"Why don't I stay for dinner," he suggested. "Or breakfast would be good too. You remember how I like my eggs?"

"Naw, that ain't gonna work for me," my mother said. "My boyfriend is comin' over tonight."

"Boyfriend?"

"Yeah, boyfriend, Roy. You know, it's like a girlfriend but it's a boy," she said. "You know all about girlfriends, don't you, Roy? My boyfriend is Napoleon Boykin."

"Napoleon? Is he a brother?"

"Yeah, like it's any of your goddamned business one way or another," she said. "Roy, nobody stopped living just 'cause you walked out."

"I can see you ain't stopped living with all these kids running around here," he said, laughing.

"Fuck you, Roy. The sun don't rise and set in your ass," she said.

"That's the old Say that I remember," he said, rising to leave.

Yvonne shuffled toward him, blocking his exit, and handed him some papers.

"What's this here?" he said, reading aloud. "This court order grants two people who want to marry consent, if they are expecting a baby."

"What's this bullshit?" my mother said, snatching the papers.

She dropped onto the sofa, head in her hands. Then she looked at Yvonne. "You pregnant, girl? When was you gonna tell me?"

"We gotta get married," Yvonne said. "And you already said you ain't gonna sign for it."

The next few days passed in a blur. Roy Randolph was over every day for a week. He and my mother were going to take Yvonne to a "girls' home," Bobby said, where she would stay until the baby was born. Then, she would give the baby up for 'doption.

"What's that?" I asked.

"That's when somebody cain't take care of their kids, so they give 'em away to somebody who can," he told me.

What a terrible idea, I thought. Families should stay together no matter what.

But Roy Randolph and my mother took Yvonne to

the girls' home and brought her right back again. Yvonne went into our room and slammed the door. Roy Randolph slammed the front door on his way out, and my mother called Uncle John, her favorite gossip buddy.

"Yeah, John, we took her," she said. "But she just acted out. She fell down on her knees and cried and cried, and begged, 'Mama, Mama, please don't let 'em take my baby.' John, it was just pathetic. I just couldn't do it...Yeah, Roy was pissed. At least that'll keep his sorry ass from comin' over here so much. He wanted to visit his little girl and play at being big pappy to the rescue but he found out he was gonna be a grandpappy instead. You know that man is stupid and vain. He don't wanna explain to all those young heffas he's running around with that he's a grandpappy."

Six months later, we had a new baby in the house— Everette Clay Doss Jr. or Little Butch. He was very cute, with wavy hair and beautiful big brown eyes. Most of his care fell to Cynthia and me. Yvonne started receiving welfare checks, which she spent on clothes for herself and Big Butch.

Otherwise, things continued much as before.

On most weekends our neighbor Bill would show up to drink and hang out with my mother. Bill could fix just about anything mechanical, we'd been told. Apparently, he only had to smell an engine to tell that a car needed oil. My mother believed that these skills surely extended to plumbing, and she offered him forty dollars and a fifth of whiskey to work on our constantly overflowing toilet. He couldn't make the situation any worse than it was, she figured.

Bill would start working on the bathroom in the morning, with a half-pint of J&B hanging out of his back pocket, and by mid-afternoon he was drunk. Still, he worked hard and succeeded in fixing our toilet. My mother asked him to fix the tub, which took a lot longer to get in working order. Until the tub was fixed, we were allowed to run the neighbor's water hose through the bathroom window and into the tub. We bailed the water out with a bucket through the same window, beneath which a permanent mud puddle was home to all sorts of bugs.

When Bill was finally done with repairs, he had replaced the tub, sink, toilet, and most of the pipes. This set off a frenzy among us kids, as we battled for who would get to use the tub first.

After the plumbing had been fixed, we started to notice other problems in the house. The roof leaked on rainy days, and we didn't have enough pots to catch it all, so the carpet was soaked in patches. The room smelled like wet diapers, and black and brown mold spots started to form on the walls.

Finally, my mother decided to confront the owner about the state of the house, and the next day she and I visited Mr. Stone's Beverly Hills office. The plush lawn-green rug matched the curtains, and the brass desk set was polished to a bright gleam. I could see my reflection in the shiny pencil holder, my forehead bulging and enormous. I was giggling at this when Mr. Stone was wheeled into the room. I had never been close to anyone in a wheelchair before, and I fell silent.

Mr. Stone's head lolled from side to side like a rag doll, but his voice came out crisp and clear.

"This is an adults-only rental, Sarah, but I made an allowance for you as far as kids were concerned," Mr. Stone said. "Your application allowed for four kids. When my man stopped by for the rent, he said that he noticed twice as many."

"Well, if there was bullshit being slung, then it was being slung on both sides of the fence," my mother said. "You said the house was a fixer-upper, but you didn't say that the plumbing was rotten and the roof was caving in."

My mother looked Mr. Stone directly in the eye. She didn't seem to take any notice of the large Black man who had wheeled him into the room. His expression suggested that he didn't like either of us very much. The brass buttons on his uniform matched the polished sheen of the desk set.

"I told you there were problems with the house. You were

desperate for a place to stay, and you rented it sight unseen as I recall," Mr. Stone said evenly. "And you signed a contract. And you have to honor your contract unless one party or another is incompetent in some way. Are you incompetent, Sarah? Because I'm sure not."

"Yeah, I signed a contract but I thought I was at least getting a place for me and my kids to take a shit."

The Black man standing behind Mr. Stone all but growled.

"It's all right, Thomas," Mr. Stone said. "You can leave us alone."

The man scowled at my mother and me and disappeared through the beaded curtain.

"What's his trip?" my mother asked.

"Thomas has been with my family for years and gets a little protective when he thinks someone is threatening me."

"I'm not threatening you, but I can. I ain't payin' no more rent until you fix the bullshit that's wrong with that damn house," my mother said. "And I don't care if I got twenty kids living up in that motherfuckah. You hear me?"

We left Mr. Stone sitting behind his desk, looking bewildered. It was my guess that most people—Black or white, but especially Black—didn't talk to him that way.

Despite our meeting with Mr. Stone, he refused to fix anything, and the mold continued to grow on the walls like black tears. We chose to ignore it. Since no rent was being paid, we were technically squatters. But no one came to evict us.

We settled into a comfortable routine. While the house had its issues, it was better than living with the Gordons, and it sure as hell beat facing Miss Mai and her girls on Ninety-Second and Avalon. Still, I sometimes thought that it wasn't as much fun as living at the Cameo movie theater downtown.

When he was sober, Bill fixed as many things as he could. He even patched some of the bigger holes in the roof. His buddy, Napoleon Boykin, helped him with the bigger jobs.

Napoleon—or Nicky, as he was called—was a squat guy with a beer belly, who giggled like a girl when amused.

He wore beanies in various colors of the rainbow and had known Bill since they'd been "back down South" together. While he and my mother were dating, Nicky didn't move in with us. He lived in a trailer park about five miles from our house. He said he couldn't live with a woman he was not married to. But that didn't keep him from spending every weekend at our house.

Finally, we were told that Nicky was moving back down South. He already had a woman with kids down there.

Some months later, I arrived home from school to learn that my mother had been rushed to Martin Luther King Jr. hospital in Watts. I was very worried because the hospital was known as Killer King in the neighborhood. There were many stories about people who checked in and never checked out. Mama had to have an emergency hernia operation, Yvonne told me.

We three girls took the bus to see our mother. As we marched through the dimly lit corridors of the hospital, Yvonne asked if we wanted to see our new baby brother and sister.

Brother and sister? I stared at her, mouth dropped open in surprise. Wasn't our mother in the hospital for a hernia operation?

"Mama didn't want nobody to know 'cause she might be giving them up for 'doption."

Another brother and sister? They were to be given up for adoption? It just couldn't be true! I ran screaming down the hallway. "Mama! Mama! Where you at?"

Yvonne said, "Shut up, girl, this here is a hospital. Don't you see them quiet signs telling you to be quiet? Mama is in room 1020."

I flew into room 1020 and saw my mother lying on the bed. "Mama, I don't have no little brother and sister, huh? Yvonne just lyin' 'bout that 'doption stuff, huh?"

My mother turned her tired face away from me, and I knew that Yvonne had been telling the truth. Cynthia entered the room quietly behind me. Instinctively, I took her hand in mine, and we walked to the hospital bed together.

"Mama, we gonna watch 'em," I said. "You don't have to put them up for no 'doption."

My mother closed her eyes and lay back on the bed. She looked so small all of a sudden.

Cynthia said, "Me and Mary is gonna watch them babies when we get home from school and before we go to school. Don't worry, Mama. We already do it for Butch. We know how to take care of a baby."

My mother's face had a look of suffering that I'd seen only once before, on our dog Jack, right after he'd had a paw crushed by a milk truck. Jack stayed under the porch for a week and wouldn't come out, even to eat.

"Now look, you stupid girl," Yvonne said. "You upset Mama."

Yvonne ushered us into the hallway. I was hysterical all the way down the hall to the NICU or Neonatal Intensive Care Unit, as the sign on the door read.

I didn't have anyone to ask what "neonatal" meant, for through the large picture window, I could see a number of crying, squirmy, blotchy babies, swaddled in incubators. They were hooked up to tubes and machines, like an array of Frankenstein's monsters.

"That's yo' brother and sister back there," Yvonne said, pointing at two babies. They were no larger than a couple of soda cans, and they were hooked up to dozens of tubes that poked from holes in their tiny bodies. I started to tremble as I peered through the glass.

The babies were half the size of my smallest baby doll at home. Somebody had to be responsible for their condition, I thought. In health class at school, we were taught that mothers who drank and smoked risked injuring their unborn babies. And my mother smoked and drank all the time.

"Mama did this to the babies?" I asked Yvonne. "At school they said whatever mothers put into their bodies, they give to their babies," I said. "Mama should have stopped smoking and drinking when she knew she was going to have a baby."

But Mama hadn't known she was pregnant, Yvonne insisted. "She's always been on the heavy side, and sometimes, when a woman is too skinny or too fat, she cain't tell if she is pregnant or not," Yvonne explained. "Them babies is premature. This is just what happens sometimes when babies are born before nine months. It ain't nobody's fault."

Yvonne parked me and Cynthia outside my mother's room. "Y'all gotta wait out here while I go in the room to talk to Ma and the doctor," Yvonne told us.

A tall white man in a lab coat hurried by me and into my mother's room. He didn't notice when I quietly slipped in behind him. My mother wasn't sharing the room with anyone, and her bed was on a far wall. The curtain was drawn, so my mother couldn't see me, and I was able to hear everything he said.

"We repaired the hernia," the doctor said. "As you know, this condition during pregnancy is really quite serious. We repaired it, and the babies are viable, but they're going to need very specialized care, perhaps even for the rest of their lives. So have you thought any more about what I suggested?"

"I don't know, Doctor," my mother said. "It might not be the best thing for my family."

"Maybe not, but it might be the best thing for these babies," the doctor said. "The twins are barely at the viability limit. We'll know more in a few weeks, but they might both require expensive long-term care and rehabilitation. Adoption might be the best way to go, if you're thinking about the welfare of the children."

"I'll let you know," my mother said weakly. "I just want to sleep now."

No one saw me as I left the room. So it's this stupid doctor who wanted to take my brother and sister away from our family, I thought.

I had never met any adopted kids as far as I knew, and everything I knew about adoption I had learned from television. In the show *Family*, Quinn Cummings played an adopted girl who was having a lot of problems. And she'd been adopted by rich white people, I thought. My little brother and sister were tiny, sick, Black babies. Why should my mother want to add to their trouble by putting them up for adoption?

My mother came home three days later but the babies, who were not yet named, did not come with her.

I knew that naming things was very important. I remembered how Big Willie kept chickens. Some he named and they were our pets, and others he told us not to name, and they were our dinner. Every night, I prayed to God that the babies would be given names and be brought home to us. Another month passed. Maybe my prayers were answered because the twins finally received names—Mark and Mariah Boykin—and came home after they had put on some weight.

We now had two new mothers in the house and three new babies. The house was never quiet. Things were worse when Yvonne and my mother argued. Now that Yvonne was a mother herself, she seemed to believe that she was on equal footing with our mother.

"Get out befo' I stomp you in the crack of the ass!" my mother yelled. Everyone ran into the living room to see who she was talking to. "You been givin' every dime of that welfare check to that good-for-nothin' nigga', and you ain't got enough money to buy yo' baby some Pampers! You got them girls usin' my babies' Pampers. And you think you gonna lie up in here and not go to school, you got another thing comin', bitch!"

My mother was throwing Yvonne's things out into a big pile on the front porch. Out went clothing, jewelry, shoes, and the stereo.

My mother told Yvonne that Little Butch could stay but she had to go. "Cain't but one woman run one house," my mother said as she slammed the door on Yvonne and her belongings. I looked out the window and Big Butch was coming across the street toward Yvonne.

"What happened, baby?" I heard him say.

"That money-hungry bitch threw me out," she said.

I immediately went to tell my mother what Yvonne had said.

"Get the fuck off my porch, Butch," my mother said through the door.

"Ain't goin' nowhere without my son," Butch said.

"You goin' if I say you goin'," my mother said.

It wasn't so much *what* she said but *how* she said it that made us know that she meant business. If my mother started to clench her teeth, that meant that she was one step away from pulling out her gun. And Yvonne well knew it. She pulled Butch away by his sleeve just as my mother walked onto the porch waving her .22 handgun.

"Give me my baby," Yvonne said, shaking and looking directly into the barrel of the gun.

My mother called me and told me to go get Little Butch. I wrapped him in a blanket. He smelled of baby oil and sour milk and looked up at me with soft brown, wide eyes. I started to cry. He did not make a sound. I shook so badly as I handed him to Yvonne that I was afraid I might drop him.

My mother didn't say another word. She slid the gun into her cleavage like it was a holster. She turned and went inside the house.

We didn't hear from Yvonne for two months. Finally, she telephoned to say that she was staying in the Nickerson Gardens Apartments, a public housing facility that my mother often referred to as the "slave quarters."

"How can you stand all of those niggas livin' stacked on top of each other?" my mother asked Yvonne.

My mother decided to invite Yvonne and Big Butch to dinner. She missed her grandson, she told them. When they arrived, it was as if the terrible argument had never taken place. We chowed down on my mother's best dish of oxtail soup and cornbread. There was Boone's Farm Apple Wine for Butch and Yvonne and whiskey for my mother. Everyone was laughing. Yvonne told my mother that the housing projects weren't as bad as she thought and that we should come for a visit soon. In fact, she invited Morris, Cynthia, and me to stay for part of the summer. My mother told her that she would think about it.

It was almost summer and for the first time in a long while, we had free time. On most days that summer, we would play in the vacant lot down the street. We had rigged up a human catapult by resting a board over a large rock like a teeter-totter. One person would stand on one end while the fattest kid on the block would jump off a kitchen chair onto the other end, propelling the skinnier kid ten feet onto a bunch of old mattresses. When it was the fat kid's turn, two people jumped off the chair together to propel him forward. Jumpers were judged by the quality of their somersaults. To us, it was just like the Olympics.

My mother didn't like this game. She said we were going to break our "fool necks" playing it. But we played it every chance we got when she wasn't looking. Perhaps she knew this and perhaps that was why she agreed to let us visit Yvonne's apartment in the "slave quarters" that summer. Perhaps she thought we'd be safer.

For Cynthia, Morris, and me, visiting Yvonne was like going away to camp, just like those white kids did in the movies. For us it was an adventure—a new place to sleep, play, and explore. My mother went with us on our first visit.

We caught the crosstown bus to the Nickerson Gardens Apartments. The "slave quarters" consisted of a collection of government-brown two-story apartments, surrounding a courtyard of concrete and patchy, dying grass.

As soon as we arrived, my mother barged in without knocking and went to Little Butch, who was sleeping in his bassinette.

"That's Nana's baby," she said, lifting him up and

inspecting him like a ripening melon. Little Butch squirmed in her arms but didn't cry. My mother blew into his belly, making a raspberry sound, and Little Butch practically screamed with laughter. She smelled his bottom, and her nose wrinkled. Then she lifted her head and sniffed the room. Another smell lingered in the room, a heavy, sweet odor like burning flowers.

"Where you keep the Pampers?" my mother called to Yvonne.

"We're out," Yvonne said. "We just been using kitchen towels and pins until I get my county check."

"You mean to tell me that you got money for reefer but not for your baby's diapers?" my mother said. "You layin' up in here with that man and playing house. He ain't workin', and you ain't workin', and neither one of y'all goin' ta school. What the hell do you do all day but watch them damn soap operas, eat, and fuck?"

"Mama, don't start," Yvonne said.

"I don't know how I raised such a weak-ass chile," my mother said. "These girls here can help you, if this baby is too much for you."

My mother reached into her bra and took out a handkerchief full of coins. "Mary, you go on down to the store and get this baby some Pampers," she said, handing me the money.

"Okay, Mama," I said. "Can Morris go with me? Can we go see the playground on the way?"

"Yeah," my mother said.

Cynthia stayed behind so she could have a turn holding Little Butch.

The playground had been reduced to a dirt hole that must have once contained a sand box, and a beaten-up metal slide with the word Piru spray-painted on it. We decided it was enough. Just as Morris was sliding down and I was poised to follow him, someone yanked me down the ladder.

"What set you from?" a light-skinned kid of about thirteen

demanded. He had blotchy red pimples on his face and a serious overbite. His upper lip completely overshadowed his lower one. His protruding forehead and sunken cheeks gave his head a skull-like appearance. "Bitch, I said, what set you from?"

I felt like Dorothy in *The Wizard of Oz* who was constantly asked if she was a good witch or a bad one. "I'm not a witch at all," I said, smiling and flashing my dimple.

"I said *bitch*, bitch," he said. "This here is Piru territory, and you cain't get up there unless we say you can get up there."

"We ain't in no stupid gang," Morris spoke up.

"You calling me stupid, punk?" the kid said. His index and middle finger disappeared in his mouth, and he let out a long, loud bird whistle.

I raced around to the front of the slide and grabbed Morris's hand. "Run!" I shouted, half dragging, half carrying Morris through the courtyard as we were pelted with rocks from behind.

When we came back without the Pampers, my mother wanted to know what had happened. We didn't tell her because that would just make a bad situation worse. We lied and said we'd been at the playground and had forgotten to go to the store. I still wanted to spend part of the summer with Yvonne, and I didn't need my mother shooting up the place.

My mother took the money from me and went to get the diapers. When she returned, she said that we could spend some time at Yvonne's house as long as we agreed to help out with Little Butch.

That night we told Big Butch about our mad dash through the courtyard. He just smiled and nodded, but the next day he insisted on accompanying us to the playground. The same kid was sitting on the end of the slide, smoking a cigarette. I wanted to tell him that he wasn't old enough to smoke, but I thought better of it.

"Hey, Red Bone," Butch said to the boy. "This here is my little brother and sister."

The kid jumped to attention as if he were a soldier addressing a superior officer. "Hey, Butch," he said. "I asked 'em what set they was from, and they didn't tell me that you was they brother. Hey, I'm sorry, man."

"It's okay," he said. "Just don't let nothin' happen to them. Ya hear?"

"Yeah, I got your back, brother man. Ain't nothin' gonna happen to 'em when I'm around."

After that we were able to use the slide whenever we wanted, and no one bothered us. In fact, the kid stepped between us and a couple of kids who wanted to beat us up. He whispered something in their ears and they walked away.

One day we were on the playground and Big Butch drove up in a sky-blue Chevy Impala. The back of the car rode very low to the ground and kicked up sparks from the street. Fuzzy dice hung from the rearview mirror and little toy dogs in the back window had heads that bobbed up and down in a neverending *yes* motion. A booming noise pulsed from the speakers, and I recognized the song "That's the Way (I Like It)."

"Get in," Butch hollered.

"Whose car is this?" I yelled. Butch said something I couldn't hear over the music. "What?" I yelled back.

Butch turned off the radio and asked, "Wanna ride?"

"Yeah!" my brother and I said at the same time.

"Just don't tell your mama," he said as we wiggled onto the front bench next to him. "This is my friend's car and I'm just driving it for the day."

Big Butch drove like a maniac through the housing complex. Morris shouted "wheeeee" as we veered dangerously close to walls and ditches. I covered my ears to block out the noise of squealing tires and the music that made my heart thump like a big animal in a small cage.

That summer Big Butch always seemed to be driving a lot

of different cars, and he would often pick us up on the playground and take us for a ride. Yvonne told me that when we rode along with him the cops probably wouldn't stop him. I asked why the cops would want to stop him, but she didn't answer me. At the end of the summer, we asked our mother if we could stay longer but she said no. School was starting soon.

I came home from my first day of fifth grade and Yvonne was sitting in our living room with several shopping bags of clothes at her feet. She had a black eye.

"I told you that good-for-nothin' nigga was gonna hit you," my mother said. "I'm gonna kill that motherfuckah when I see him."

"Can I stay?" Yvonne asked. My mother nodded, and Yvonne and Little Butch were back to live with us.

It was as if they had never left. We didn't see Big Butch for weeks. Then one day, when we were walking home from the ABC market loaded down with groceries, he appeared on the street corner. He walked over to my mother, Yvonne, and me, as if nothing had happened.

"Hey, baby, let me talk to you a minute," he said to Yvonne.

"Boy, if you don't get away from here—" my mother said. She didn't finish her threat but dropped her bags on the sidewalk; one of them spilled orange juice onto the pavement. I thought my mother was going to go for the gun concealed in her bra, but instead she pulled out some scissors from her purse, and pointed them at his crotch, making it clear what she would like to do to him.

"Come on, Mama," he said. "I just wanna talk to my girl." My mother, placing her bulk in front of me and Yvonne, held the scissors in front of her and glared at Big Butch. "Okay, okay, Mama," he said. "I ain't tryin' ta start no trouble. But I do wanna see my son."

Yvonne spoke up behind her. "You can come see Little Butch this weekend," she said.

My mother raised her eyebrows at Yvonne, and Yvonne

looked back with a blank expression. We started gathering the groceries off the sidewalk.

That Saturday Big Butch came to visit and afterwards my mother persuaded Yvonne to leave Little Butch with us.

"You go on out there and get yourself serviced," she said. "Then you come back and be a mama to your boy."

Big Butch did not object, and we saw them often enough. The two of them went to his mother's house every day to eat. She was right next door, so Yvonne would stop in and visit with Little Butch.

On one such visit, I asked her why she would go back to someone who had hit her.

"You just a kid and you don't know nothin' about love," she said. "Big Butch was just high that day that we got into that fight. Mama would say that love covers all sins."

I wanted to tell her that love covers a multitude of sins, which is different from "all sins." And the Bible didn't say anything about letting some man hit on you. But I didn't say a word. She wasn't going to listen to me.

One day I saw Big Butch sawing a piece of wood in his mother's backyard. I asked him what he was doing, and he said he was making a gun. "Outta wood?" I asked.

"Yeah, it's a zip gun," he said. "I gotta protect myself."

The wooden object had the shape of a gun, with a thick rubber band on the top and a metal pipe. I told Yvonne, worried that Butch might be making the gun to use on Mama.

"You don't know nothin' 'bout nothin', girl," she said. "Them Crips been after him."

While it may have looked like a gun, it didn't function as one. It wasn't long before we heard that the gun had exploded in Butch's hand, almost splitting it in two.

After his hand was sewn back together, Butch would need months of physical therapy—or so his friends told us when they stopped by to tell Yvonne about the accident. My mother said we should go visit Big Butch in the hospital.

"The scriptures say you reap what you sow and that's

God's justice," my mother said. "But it also say that your heavenly father will forgive you as you forgive those who sin against you."

My mother invited Butch to dinner when he got out of the hospital, and he stayed with us for the next two months. So it was no surprise to discover that Yvonne was expecting again. Tammy—spelled "Tamie" because of Yvonne's reading deficiency—was born just after Yvonne's eighteenth birthday.

Yvonne ignored the new baby and started following Butch everywhere. It was as if she couldn't leave him alone, no matter how badly he treated her. And he didn't marry her, even after he no longer needed our mother's consent. It turned out that Butch had another girl on the side, a girl, even "slower" than Steven, who was rumored to be giving him money to stay with her.

This was too much for Yvonne, so she started dating Big Butch's best friend, Michael Pitts. She moved into Michael Pitts's mama's house and even started calling that woman Mommy. The neighborhood rumor was that the Pittses were the biggest pill dealers on the block. Mrs. Pitts gave Yvonne plenty of methamphetamines, which gave my sister enough energy to clean her house. People said that Mrs. Pitts sometimes hired Yvonne out as a maid to other people in the neighborhood.

Meanwhile, my mother added Tamie to the household brood and told Yvonne to stay away until she came to her senses.

So we had two more mouths to feed during the tough times that followed. Welfare cut us off when my mother went to work as a nurse's aide, the same month that the employees of Kaiser Permanente Hospital—where my mother worked—went on strike. When the strike fund dried up, my mother applied for welfare again, but she was told that she had to file a new application, and that it would take ten working days to process.

The little food we had to eat was filched from our school lunches and brought home to share with the little ones who were not yet old enough to go to school. Over the weekend there was nothing to eat.

We had not eaten for two days when my mother borrowed ten dollars from her friend Bill, and bought a fifty-pound sack of potatoes and a two-pound brick of lard from the Avocado Corner Farmer's Market. We lived on french fries for a week until our welfare check came. Then we were officially "on the county."

The checks arrived on the first and fifteenth of each month. Most of the kids in the neighborhood were "on the county." The mailman had become a local hero of sorts at least twice a month. The kids on our street would wait for the mail carrier with the same breathless anticipation that we had reserved for the ice-cream truck. As a group we followed him to each mailbox. In our family we received $375 every two weeks in welfare payments. A few days after the welfare checks arrived, we received $175 in food stamps.

Even though the checks were coming on a regular basis now, we still found ourselves scrounging for something to eat at the end of each month. Morris and I were determined to take matters into our own hands. We had spent all morning hustling up return-deposit bottles, when we heard that ten-pound bags of potatoes were on sale at the supermarket for thirty-nine cents. We still had a pound of lard in the refrigerator and were lucky enough to find two empty RC cola bottles in a vacant lot. Their return value was twenty cents. We checked the paper machines and the telephone booths for stray change and came up with another two dimes. The ten-pound bag of spuds lasted at least a day, maybe more.

Everyone in my family knew how to make french fries. Give any one of us a sharp knife, and we could cut up a potato in twenty seconds flat. We made a game of it. Cynthia was the fastest at ten seconds.

My mother had long since pawned most of her guns,

including the .22-caliber pistol that she used to carry in her bra, which was unfortunate because of what happened on one county check day.

"We was gettin' off the bus on Broadway, and these three boys just ran up and snatched my purse," she told us. "I took some cans from the shopping bags, and I started pitching them at the little motherfuckahs," she said. "A few landed on their heads, and I thought they was gonna drop the purse. Then I turned around and one of the little bastards had Willie," she said, referring to my ten-year-old brother. "Willie was trying to hit him, but the guy was holding him in a headlock. They said, 'Lady, just stop throwin' those damn cans and we'll let him go.' So I stopped throwin'. Boy, if I'd had my .22 that day, it would have been a different story."

My mother never got her purse back or any of the other five purses that were snatched off her shoulder on county check day over the years. You would think the muggers would've figured out that she didn't carry valuables in her purse. Cash, food stamps, and her California ID were rolled up in a handkerchief and stuffed in her bra. Her purses contained lipstick, bus fare tokens, Certs, Bugler Tobacco for roll-your-own cigarettes, handkerchiefs, and the latest novel she was reading.

Sometimes during the lean months we even exhausted our store of potatoes. It was during those times that my mother's friend Bill offered to take us junking for scrap metal, bottles, aluminum cans, and cardboard.

I asked my mother if I could go "junking" with her. I was always amazed at the things people threw away, especially in areas like Beverly Hills. Once while "junking" I found a whole Barbie doll with her clothes on. Her hair was a little singed, and her head was a little melted. I guessed that someone had taken a match to her hair. Maybe because she was injured, she became my favorite doll.

Morris and I were the best "junkers" in the family after my mother, and West Park was the best place to hustle bottles, particularly if there had been a sports activity that day. People drank lots of soda, but mostly beer, when they were playing soccer or baseball.

Morris and I went to work. He laced his fingers together and hoisted me into the large garbage bins. I flipped over into the dumpster and reached back for him, pulling him up by his T-shirt. Our "junking" outfits consisted of clothing we had outgrown or that had rips in it. We each wore a pair of my mother's gardening gloves. They were too big but kept our hands from being cut on broken glass or tin can tops. Each of us had sticks with nails hammered into them, which were useful for rooting through really disgusting things like loaded Pampers, dead cats, or dead rats.

There must have been a soccer game that day, because the dumpster was full of empty beer cans, and they were right at the top of the garbage, which meant that the game had only recently broken up. The dumpsters at the park were only a few blocks from our house, and I didn't want the neighbors to see us "dumpster diving."

One day I was humiliated when a girl I knew spotted me in a dumpster. Her name was Lorelei Meadows, and I hated her. She was the most popular girl in the sixth grade and she always wore the best clothes.

"Mary Hill?" she screamed across the park. "Is that you?"

I recognized her voice immediately, and I dove into the garbage face first. Morris just peeked over the side, and I pulled him down next to me. My nose was right next to a dead rat. I held my breath. Lorelei peered over the edge of the can. She was also popular because she was the tallest girl in school and a star on the basketball team.

"What you doin' in there?" she asked.

"I'm just playin' hide and seek," I said.

"Yeah, right," she said, laughing as she walked away.

Of course, everyone heard about it at school, where I was already unpopular for a number of reasons: I was quick to remind the teacher that we had homework, I didn't dress

well, and I didn't participate in the Pledge of Allegiance. I
didn't feel as if I had any control over any of this. The homework was due, after all, and I thought I was helping everyone
by reminding the teacher of it. I didn't dress well because
most of my clothing was hand-me-downs from Cynthia or
Yvonne. Nothing fit. Yvonne was four sizes larger than me,
and Cynthia was two sizes smaller. I must have always looked
like I was gaining and losing weight overnight. As for the
Pledge of Allegiance, that was my mother's idea. She said
that reciting the Pledge was like saying a prayer to the state,
and we owed God's things to God.

Once when I was in fourth grade, the teacher noticed that
I wasn't participating in the Pledge of Allegiance and insisted
that I recite it along with everyone else. When I shook my
head, he told me to stand outside the classroom in the rain,
saying his son was risking his life in Vietnam and we needed
to support the boys overseas.

I wasn't allowed to go home and change, and I walked
around all day wet. When the last bell rang, I tore out the
front door and ran all the way home, arriving breathless and
damp.

"I'm sayin' the Pledge tomorrow," I told my mother.

"No, you ain't," she said.

"Mr. Wheatly made me stand in the rain," I said. "I could
have drowned!"

Instead of grabbing her gun and going down to the school
and shooting Mr. Wheatly for nearly killing me, my mother
just smiled. She said, "Think of all the things that the son of
God suffered for his father's truth, and then complain to me
about being a little damp."

It was definitely something to think about. After that, I
dutifully stood outside the classroom every time the Pledge
was recited—rain or shine.

My mother taught me to recite the Lord's Prayer instead.
So when the kids inside the classroom were saying "I pledge
allegiance to the flag of the United States of America..." I

was outside mumbling, "Our father who art in heaven, hallowed be thy name…"

My mother decided we should start attending the Kingdom Hall so that I could learn to properly worship the true God. But it was not something that could be forced, she said. "Jehovah don't want no robots," she said.

I figured that anybody who could get my mother to see that people—even kids—needed to make their own choices sometimes couldn't be all bad. I volunteered to go to the meeting with her.

"Matthew 9:37 shows there is a need for workers in righteousness because God says that the harvest is plentiful but the workers are few," my mother said.

We took the crosstown bus to the Kingdom Hall on Avalon, just a few blocks away from Miss Mai and her girls. I tried to pull my jacket over my head so as not to be recognized.

"What if Miss Mai or her girls are here?" I asked as we approached the entrance.

"If they are, then that's a good thing," my mother said. "It's a place where the lion lies down with the lamb."

Great, I thought, *but I would still rather be a lion than a lamb.*

The Hall was sparsely decorated. We were under strict instructions not to call it a church. A church refers to a congregation of people, my mother explained, but the Hall was a building where people who wanted to preach the word of Jehovah God met for meetings and Bible study. Twenty rows of green upholstered chairs faced a small stage with a podium in a windowless room.

Six ceiling fans revolved overhead. There were no candles, no stained glass, no crosses, and no collection plate to be seen. All donations were discreetly accepted in the rear in two locked wooden boxes. Brass plaques on the boxes read "Worldwide Work and Congregation Local Expenses." Passing around a basket for donations was something that they did in "pagan" churches, my mother explained. "If their gods are so powerful, then why do you think they are always broke?" she asked me. Witnesses accepted donations, she told me, but they didn't shake you down like some churches did. Mormons kept a running tally, and if you weren't paid up with ten percent of your wages, you couldn't go to their temple.

At the Kingdom Hall, the congregation was mixed. It was a Black neighborhood but Mexicans, Blacks, and whites attended as well. We had our share of Mexican families in South Central, but almost no whites lived there. For the first time I thought how rare it was to see a white person outside of television. If you did spot one, they were usually cops, teachers, or social workers, or they were just lost. At the Kingdom Hall there were a few white people sprinkled here and there among the congregation.

Music played before every meeting. On this occasion the song was called "Life Without End—At Last!" There was no choir, so everyone sang along. I had been to the Hall only a few times so I didn't know the words. An old man next to me shared his songbook. He placed his finger on each line that we were supposed to sing. My mother sang from memory. Her voice was gravelly and deep like a man's, but she was at least on key.

Some voices were clearly better than others, but the good voices carried the bad ones.

We sang as one.

After the song was over, a white man in a pressed blue suit began a lecture that was called "the main talk." He said, "A physical man can only receive the things that are physical. But a spiritual man examines all things both physical and spiritual, and this is in harmony with 1 Corinthians: 2:11, 14, and 15. God's Kingdom will abundantly provide for the needs of all of its subjects, as we can see in Isaiah 40:26 and Psalms 145:16. Regardless of your nationality, you have the opportunity to become a subject of God's Kingdom."

My mother took copious notes and quickly found the

reference scriptures in the Bible. I had never before seen my mother so interested and focused. She answered so many questions during the Bible-study portion that they had been forced to start calling on someone else.

After the meeting I suggested that we walk the three blocks to Miss Mai's house and tell her about the meeting. My mother smiled and placed a few dollars in the Worldwide Work box.

"She might not be ready to hear this from us," my mother said. "At the next meeting we'll tell the elders to send someone to her apartment."

Six

Black Power, Real Life, and the Imitation of Life

Weeks went by, but we did not return to the Kingdom Hall. In the meantime, my mother had met a new man. Anderson Taylor was not a Jehovah's Witness but a member of the Black Muslims or Nation of Islam. His group sold bean pies on street corners to raise money. The pies were made from cooked, mashed navy beans and tasted a little like sweet potato pie.

My mother had initially brought Anderson home to meet Yvonne, who visited us most weekends. Anderson was ten years older than Yvonne and fifteen years younger than my mother.

My mother had met Anderson at the public library. He didn't wear a suit coat and bow tie like other members of the Nation of Islam but always appeared in a black karate gi that he let hang open to expose his smooth, finely sculptured chest. Yvonne, however, was completely uninterested. "He is always talking about that Black Power shit," she said.

When my mother introduced him to us, he bowed and said, "*As-Salaam-Alaikum.*" We laughed.

"What's that you say about selling us a Cadillac?" Bobby cracked.

"This is a traditional greeting," Anderson said. "It means 'may peace be with you.'"

"Did Yvonne call?" my mother asked.

"Yeah, and she said she ain't goin' nowhere with this weird dude," Bobby said.

Anderson seemed unfazed. "I guess I'll have to take out your lovely mother instead," he said.

He extended his arm to my mother, just like in one of those old movies, and they walked out together. In less than a week, Anderson had moved in with us. While he couldn't persuade my mother to go to the Muslim temple with him, she stopped going to the Kingdom Hall on the weekends. She stopped wearing makeup and wore long, unflattering dresses that covered her like stitched blankets. She stopped buying pork chops and ham because Anderson said that, according to Allah, the pig was an unclean beast.

As for Yvonne, she barely spoke to Anderson when she visited. Despite having rejected him first, she couldn't understand why he would prefer my mother to her.

We asked Anderson what kind of work he did, and he told us that he was a movie stunt double for the Black martial arts superstar Jim Kelly, who had appeared as the only Black character in a few martial arts movies.

Anderson disappeared for several days of the month, claiming he was auditioning for martial arts films.

One weekend we all went to the latest *Black Belt Jones* movie, starring Jim Kelly. Anderson had told us that he was the stunt double for Kelly, and that if we looked closely, we would see that it was him in the final scene—and not Kelly—who was kicked through a wall. We couldn't see it. I suggested that we stay and read the credits, but all of a sudden Anderson was in a big hurry to get home.

Anderson said that when he hit it big he was going to buy a Corvette and a house in Palos Verdes. Our family, we noticed, never figured into his fantasies of success. We started calling him The Dreamer.

Ainey heard him talking this way, but she didn't call him The Dreamer, as we did. She called him the Panther, as in the Black Panthers. And Anderson referred to her as PITA. We asked him what it stood for and he said, "Pain in the Ass."

He didn't like the fact that Ainey showed up every Friday and expected my mother to go with her to the Lobby Inn, the local bar. And he didn't like the fact that my mother would

talk to Ainey about their relationship. A typical conversation
went something like this:

"What da hell is wrong with the Panther? Why cain't you
wear makeup?"

My mother said, "He said I don't need it. I still wear a little
lipstick."

"Every woman need something, Say," Ainey said. "I got
me more wigs than Cher. He just don't want no other man to
look at you. That's what that's about. And why in the hell he
got you wrapping your hair up all the time like some mam-
my-ass bullshit?"

"This ain't mammy shit. These are wraps from Africa,"
my mother said, touching her kinte-cloth head wrap. "He
buys them over at the swap meet, and he wants me to wear
'em. He's into this whole back-to-Africa thing. No big deal.
Sometimes Black men get onto this thing because they ain't
got nothin' else to hold on to in America."

"You know the gubment be watchin' them Panther types,
Say," Ainey said. "He gonna wind up in jail and take you with
him."

"He ain't no Panther. How many times do I gotta tell
you?"

Ainey sucked her teeth, rolled her eyes, and left.

Anderson was not a Black Panther. I asked him once and I
believed him when he said he wasn't. In fact, the entire family
was present when Anderson told us that the Panthers were a
bunch of "pansy-ass pussies."

It was May 1974, and we were watching our nineteen-inch
black-and-white rented TV. Dr. George had just finished telling us it was going to be another great sunny day in California,
when an announcer broke in to talk about a house that was
being surrounded by police in South Central L.A.

It looked familiar.

"Didn't we used to live right next door to that place?"
Bobby said. "That was one of the houses we lived in before
the house that got torched."

"Yeah, I can see our porch," my mother said.

"It's something about the SLA," Anderson said. "Be quiet."

But of course, I couldn't contain myself. "What's the SLA?" I asked.

"Those are the people that are better than those pansy-ass, pussy Panthers," he said. "That's the Symbionese Liberation Army that they talkin' 'bout. Them some bad ass motherfuckahs. Now be quiet!"

We listened as the ABC news told us that a resident of the house had kidnapped Patty Hearst and were now in a shootout with the police. It seemed as if hundreds, or thousands, of people were on the street near our old house. And there were more cops than I'd ever seen in one place.

"Them is some real-ass militants. They is fightin' against the corporate fascist state," Anderson said.

I didn't know what he was getting at and I had been shushed so often that I thought I would just watch the TV and try to figure out what was going on. Then, suddenly, gunfire sounded on TV and the house caught fire.

I was scared for the people on the street. And I was scared for us. What if those cops decided that every Black person was dangerous and they just started shooting at us? There were kids out on that street. Would they shoot the kids too? I wondered. Anderson had told us the cops had beaten up a pregnant woman and were responsible for starting the Watts Rebellion. What if the cops had heard what Anderson had been saying? What if the cops came and surrounded the house we lived in now?

"They ain't gonna come ta get us, is they?" I asked Anderson.

"Naw, the SLA just want to get the pigs and all those white motherfuckahs that are takin' advantage of all the not-white people," he said. "And they tryin' to get all those political prisoners released that the white man got locked up in the prisons in this country."

The SLA was supposed to be made up of Black freedom fighters, the good guys who stood up against the whites, who were all bad; but according to the news, some white people were also members of the SLA. So, were some white people good and some white people bad? I wondered.

The next day, Anderson read the *Herald Examiner* out loud to my mother at the kitchen table. "'Six SLA members died in a two-hour shootout at a house in Los Angeles' predominantly Black South Central L.A. neighborhood. Police were relieved to discover that Patty Hearst was not among the dead.'" Anderson stopped reading for a moment. He looked up at my mother. "What the fuck is this 'relieved to discover' bullshit?" he asked. "Six good people died in there. And all they worried about is Pasty Patty."

"I'm not sure they was all good up in that house," my mother said. "They wouldn't have shot up the whole neighborhood if they was. If we still lived next door, I don't think they woulda cared if we'd all gotten shot. And the paper cares about that Hearst girl because her people own the newspaper."

Anderson rolled his eyes, and read on: "'The shootout attracted a crowd of 10,000 people. Hundreds of police officers were on hand, mostly to handle the crowd. The SWAT team used thousands of rounds on the house. It caught fire when tear gas ignited an ammunition cache inside the house. Four SLA members died inside, and two were killed in a shootout as they attempted to escape.'"

Anderson stopped reading. He tossed the paper across the table. "People are so damned stupid," he said. "They could have had the revolution right there with all those people in the streets. What in the hell were they waiting for?"

"You weren't there," I piped up. "Maybe they were waiting for you."

"Okay now," my mother said to me. "Don't let yo' mouth write a check yo' ass cain't cash."

"You know that's some bullshit," Anderson said, ignoring

me. "Those cops burned down that house with the people inside. And they executed those revolutionaries."

"Revolutionaries?" I asked.

"Yeah, like white folks claim that they celebrate on the Fourth of July."

"Oh, you mean people like Thomas Jefferson and George Washington," I said, proudly showing off my recent history lesson.

"Them ain't no revolutionaries!" Anderson screamed. "Those so-called Founding Fathers ain't nothin' but a bunch of slave-owning white pigs."

"That's not what Mr. Wheatly told us," I said. "He said it wouldn't be no country without them. He said that we all here because of them. He said they was heroes. I bet you wouldn't see them shootin' up no houses and kidnapping people."

"What kind of brainwashing-ass bullshit is they teachin' this chile?" Anderson asked my mother. "Don't you care that they don't have enough respect for our history to tell her that slaves *were* kidnapped people, and those white bastards used to keep us as property? Don't you have enough sense to teach her that a woman's place is in the struggle?"

My mother sighed heavily and glared at me. "That's enough," she said. "You stay out of grown folks' conversation."

The next day at school I repeated the entire conversation to Mr. Wheatly. He called my mother to pick me up. As I sat at my assigned desk in the classroom, my mother came in and sat across from Mr. Wheatly. I was careful not to look up at my mother. It would be like looking into the sun, I thought.

"Mrs. Gordon," Mr. Wheatly began, "I'm charged with not just educating your children. I'm charged with trying to make good citizens. We have to work together on this."

"How is she not a good citizen?" my mother said. "She's never even missed a day of school. She gets good grades.

She's always on time. And she told me that she has to remind you half the time to collect the homework."

"Perfect attendance and timely schoolwork are not the only criterion for making good citizens," he said. "Mary shows a lot of promise. But she has some strange ideas about how the world works, and it's going to get her in trouble somewhere down the line. I need you to work with me on this thing."

"What do you mean?"

"Mrs. Gordon, after our lesson on the Founding Fathers, Mary told everybody in the class that they were nothing more than slave owners," he said.

"You mean that *ain't* true?" my mother said.

"Yes, it's true that some of them owned slaves, but it's more complicated than that."

"Okay then, make it simple," my mother said.

He sighed heavily and went on. "We try to teach children to love and respect our country and the people who bled to create it. If students don't respect our country, they won't be good Americans."

"Maybe this country ought to do more to *earn* the respect of *all* of its people, not just the people who run the show," my mother said. "I don't get why my girl is in trouble for speaking the truth. Do you want to teach her just one side of the story?"

"Mrs. Gordon, there are not different sides to history," he said. "History is made up of facts."

"No, history is made by people," she said. "Some good and some bad."

The conversation ended there. "Good day, Mrs. Gordon," he said by way of dismissing her. "I have many papers to grade," he said as he walked us to the door.

On the bus ride home, my mother didn't even look at me. When we got in the house, she finally spoke. "Don't go puttin' the family business out in the streets," she told me. "I know you smart enough to know this. You ain't got to all the time tell people what you know, especially white folks. Don't go looking for trouble. It'll find you. Now go play."

But I didn't go out to play. There was a beat-up old green sofa on the porch, spewing cotton and springs. I found a flat part and I sat down. What was evil? Was it evil that some old white guys thought that they could own Black people? Was it evil for Black people to fight for freedom if it meant shooting up a neighborhood? Why did people—Black or white—want to hurt each other?

Just then, someone kicked a ball onto the porch, and I forgot about everything as I tossed it back. There was a game starting and I was the best kicker in the neighborhood.

Later that summer, Anderson and my mother got into a huge fight. I was awakened at six a.m. by shouts and screams in the living room. My mother had the phone with the long cord, and Yvonne was on the extension, standing right next to her, both of them screaming into the phone.

"You better come and get your bullshit out of my house," my mother said.

"Yeah, and I hope you bring that ho with you so we can put another hole in her ass," Yvonne said.

"You better come tonight or I'm gonna have myself a nice barbecue with all yo shit," my mother said. "You ain't gonna have me *and* some other bitch. Who da fuck you think you is? Ali Baba or some shit?"

"Yeah, we puttin' yo shit out right now," Yvonne said. "You hear that, bitch. I know you on the extension over there."

My mother looked wide-eyed and dropped the phone.

"I knew you was on the phone, bitch," Yvonne said. "I hope you do come yo crazy ass over here, 'cause my mother just went to get her gun. Ain't nobody no fucking Mormons in this house. You cain't have no—what do the crazy hos call it?—sister wives? Pimps calls they bitches that too, just so you know. And I don't care what you say that some Muslim men got more than one wife. You stupid ass stank cock ho!"

Yvonne slammed the phone down, then ran to the extension my mother had dropped and slammed that down too.

My mother put Anderson's duffel bag full of dashikis and karate gis in his old Chevy Impala. The car was the color of primer paint with patches of green. Rust streaked along the left side. As for all of the long African blanket dresses and matching head scarves that Anderson had bought my mother, they burned rather well on the barbecue pit out back, sending up plumes of smoke that smelled like burning hair all over the neighborhood.

A week later I came home from school to discover that his old Chevy had gone from the driveway. No one spoke of him after that. We went to see the *Black Belt Jones* movie a few times and looked for Anderson getting kicked through the wall but never spotted him. His name wasn't in the credits, and I concluded that he must have lied.

For the week following the African-dress barbecue, my mother spent a great deal of time sitting next to the phone. She had returned to her old habit of biting the tips off matches and spitting the strikers into an ashtray. She chewed the paper part as if it were candy. She took a black bobby pin out of her head and began to dig furiously in her right ear with it. She folded her arms, unfolded them, then picked up the receiver and dialed.

"Hello," she said. "Do this line got service or not…? Oh." She hung up.

I hated to see her like this. "If Anderson don't call, then you should call him," I told her.

"Ain't nobody waiting for no call from Anderson," she said. "Why you think I wanna talk to that dumb-ass man? He made his choice. I'm waitin' to hear from my brother. I ain't heard from John in a week. I been calling him and he don't pick up."

"Did you call his job?"

"Yeah, they just said he had a lot of vacation time built up, and he probably just took it."

She flipped through the phone book and started calling numbers, her finger yanking the holes in the rotary phone with more force with each new number dialed. I thought she would poke a hole right through the phone.

After she had called about a dozen numbers, she slammed the phone down.

"Where in the hell is that man? I've called every bar, hospital, and police station I can think of," she said. Then her eyes closed, and she swallowed hard. "The only place left is the morgue."

My mother made a few more calls from the extension in her bedroom. When she emerged, she said she had to catch the bus to USC hospital. I asked to come but she said no.

She was gone for two hours, and when she arrived home, she slumped into the sofa and didn't move for several minutes. Finally, she reached over, picked up the phone, and dialed.

"Yeah, Lo'." My mother's voice was a rough whisper. "I just came back from the USC morgue. John is there. They said he was there for a week because they found him naked in a hotel room, and they didn't know who to call. Yeah, I know. I just described him to them and they said they had a Negro John Doe fitting that description. That's what they called him, Lo', 'a Negro John Doe.'" My uncle must have asked why Uncle John wasn't wearing any clothes. My mother continued, "Hell, Lo', how in the hell should I know? Both you crazy motherfuckahs always chasing after some loose chippy. They said he probably got trick-rolled, and the ho took his clothes. Jesus, Lo', he didn't even have Daddy's watch."

Then my mother cried—something I'd only ever seen her do twice before. She had cried once, after a newscaster broke into my cartoons announcing the death of Dr. Martin Luther King Jr. in Memphis, Tennessee. She cried a second time while watching *Imitation of Life*, a movie in which a woman, who had passed for white, threw herself on the funeral carriage of her Black mother.

My mother dropped the phone, put her head in her hands, and cried big heaving sobs, coughing loudly between wails. I picked up the receiver.

"It's me, Uncle Lo'," I said. "Yeah, Mama is here but she cain't get on the phone right now. She's got morning."

"You mean she's grieving, mourning?"

"Yeah. Can you come over?"

He said he could and I hung up the phone.

For the first time in my life, I didn't want to be in the middle of grown-folk conversation. I patted my mother on her shoulder, as she had done for me so many times when I had fallen or danced too close to the stove. I think the pats helped me more than they helped her. My mother continued to cough and sob.

Ainey and Uncle Lo' came over. They drank, cried, and laughed, their conversation punctuated by threats of lawsuits against the hotel where Uncle John had been found and against the hospital where they had listed him as a "Negro John Doe."

And Uncle Lo' was particularly angry that Uncle John's watch was missing.

"That was Papa's watch," he sobbed. "They don't know what happened to Papa's watch! It's supposed to be with his family. It's supposed to come to the oldest son. That's me now!"

It was a few days before my mother was able to arrange the funeral. My mother said that Uncle John's ex-wife, Sherlyn, was "completely useless" in the planning of anything. We had been instructed to wear black for the funeral, but of course, Ainey wore red. She said she didn't own a black dress. "Too depressing," she said. Uncle Lo' busied himself hugging all the women, maybe a little too tightly.

"Grieving women are ready to just drop their panties," Uncle Lo' told Bobby.

For a moment, I thought Ainey would get into it with Uncle Lo', but she was on her best behavior.

My mother wanted a Jehovah's Witness funeral for her brother, but Sherlyn said "nuts to that." She was a Baptist, and Uncle John, she said, "ain't believed in that Witness shit since he was a boy."

My mother didn't tell Aint Sherlyn that Uncle John would have wanted a Jehovah's Witness funeral, or that stuff about Uncle John "looking down on us from heaven" would have infuriated him. My mother didn't tell her that the dead are not conscious of anything at all, or that as far as she knew, Uncle John was not among those who had "had a heavenly hope."

My mother, in a black cotton dress that reached all the way down to her ankles, just sat silently as the preacher droned on.

After the service, we filed past the coffin. In life he had preferred checkerboard sport coats with patches on the sleeves. But someone—probably my mother—had chosen to bury him in a dark blue suit with a red-and-blue-striped tie. It was strange to see him without his usual porkpie hat, his glasses, and his pipe. He looked peaceful, as if he were taking a nap. I thought of Aint Dorothy, dying alone in a mental hospital. Her clothes had been sent to Goodwill, and she'd likely been buried in a hospital gown.

Uncle John wore a bulky black watch with white numerals. It must have been my grandfather's watch that Uncle Lo' had mentioned. Uncle Lo' didn't seem to notice the watch, and I wondered why my mother had chosen to bury him with it. My mother had searched Uncle John's studio apartment for his will but couldn't find it. She told me later that that was when she had discovered Uncle John's watch. She'd wanted Uncle John to be buried with it because Uncle Lo' would have sold it and spent the money on his favorite trio of wine, women, and song. As long as the watch was on Uncle John's wrist at least the family would know where it was, she said.

After the funeral, my mother and Sherlyn searched Uncle John's studio apartment again and finally discovered his will.

In it he said he wanted a service at the Kingdom Hall, but my mother said that is "all water under the bridge now and there was no need to discuss it."

The pension from his job as a clerk typist for the County of Los Angeles amounted to $21,000. He left a third to my mother and two-thirds to his ex-wife and daughter. After my mother paid her share of the funeral expenses, she was left with $3,000. It was more money than she had ever had at one time. She gave each of us kids $100 cash, more money than we had ever had before. My mother told us that Uncle John would have wanted us to have it.

With her money my mother "caught up on bills" and purchased a used car, a white 1969 Chevy Impala. We had never had a family car before—the RTD had suited most of our needs. Besides that, I wasn't quite sure that my mother knew how to drive. She named the car Nellybelle, after a jeep she'd seen on the Roy Rogers TV show when she was a kid.

With my share I purchased tickets to the best field trips offered by my school, which included Disneyland, Knott's Berry Farm, and Lion Country Safari. I was especially eager to go to the safari park, having long been fascinated by stories of people who went through the lion preserve with their car windows down and got mauled. Unfortunately, nothing so interesting happened on our trip, but it was nice to see some lions anyway.

My oldest brother Steven gave his money to Cynthia. He said he had everything he needed. Cynthia used that $200 to throw a picnic for all the kids in the neighborhood aged ten and under. Yvonne bought clothes and pot with her money. Bobby used his share to buy magazines that he claimed "only a growing boy" could appreciate—some with giant muscle men, like Arnold Schwarzenegger, on the covers, and others featuring half-naked women.

When I asked Bobby about it, he rolled his eyes. "Women who look like that only go out with men who look like this," he said, pointing from one cover to the other.

I still didn't get it.

My younger brother Morris spent his money on comic book subscriptions, and very soon the house was littered with issues of *Superman*, the *Fantastic Four*, *She-Hulk*, *Spiderman*, and *X-Men*.

I asked him if I could read one where Superman was fighting some of the X-Men. "Girls are so stupid," he replied scornfully. "One is Marvel and the other is the D.C. universe."

I still didn't get it.

Willie purchased a small black-and-white TV with his money and used to watch it from beneath a blanket. From under the blanket, I could hear a deep voice saying that "there is nothing wrong with your television set..." and "you were about to experience the awe and mystery that reaches from the inner mind to the Outer Limits."

Teresa spent her money on every sort of treat from the ice-cream truck that paraded up and down our street twice a day, announcing its presence by blaring "Pop Goes the Weasel." Teresa did not share her treats.

Mark and Mariah were toddlers, so my mother said she was going to hold their money for them until they were older.

My mother, in the meantime, had still not driven Nellybelle, although she referred to it as if it were a new pet and lavished care on it. "I have to go wash Nellybelle," she'd say. Or, "I have to get a cover for Nellybelle."

The car sat in the driveway for more than a month before my mother decided to take it out for a spin. Bobby and I decided that we were the right co-pilots. He called shotgun and I rode in the back. As my mother revved the engine, it screeched like a cat with its tail caught in the screen door. Then, my mother just sat. The engine noise became a soft hum.

"What ya waitin' for?" Bobby asked.

My mother didn't answer him, her face expressionless. I leaned over the front seat and noticed she had her left foot on the brake and her right foot on the gas. Her hands gripped the steering wheel, as if she were wringing out clothes. Sweat ran down her right temple. She was so still that I couldn't tell if she was breathing.

I knew how she felt—it reminded me of the time my cousin Ricky had made me swim and I thought I was going to drown.

Now, looking at my mother, I knew she needed to just do it and not think about it so much. "Let's go for a drive," I said.

My mother turned over the ignition of the running engine and we scrunched further down into our seats at the screeching sound of metal on metal.

"Sorry," she said as she put the car in reverse, then slammed on the brakes. Finally, she put the car in drive and we made our way haltingly around the neighborhood.

Several times my mother put her right arm out to prevent Bobby from pitching forward through the windshield. In the rear seat my head knocked on the roof, and I had to remind myself not to swear in front of my mother. When we got back home Bobby leapt out of the car as if he were leaping from a burning building.

"That's it for me," he announced as he ran into the house.

"Mama, let's go for a drive someplace every day," I said.

My mother smiled. Once I had received a school report card on which my teacher had written, I'm proud of Mary. Below that my mother wrote, I am also proud of my Mary.

I wanted to give my mother a card that said I'm proud of you. Instead, I just acted as if the whole thing had been no big deal, as I knew she wanted me to.

That summer we drove everywhere together. We drove to the library on Avalon, about a mile from our house. We drove to my Great Uncle Sam's place, about ten miles away, and once we drove all the way to Venice Beach, a distance of thirty miles. But mostly my mother just drove to the grocery store when the food stamps arrived on the first and

fifteenth of the month. She called me her "little co-pilot."
When we went shopping, I always got something special
like a Snowball Hostess Cake, cream-filled chocolate cakes
covered with marshmallow frosting and coconut flakes. I
liked the pink ones best, although they tasted the same as the
white ones.

I would toss my mother's favorite candies—peanut brittle
and almond roca—into the basket. Those drives were our
special time together. My brothers and sisters were jealous,
but they refused to ride with my mother. Bobby said he would
not get in the car with my mother as long as she insisted on
driving with both feet.

Nellybelle broke down frequently in our second year of car
ownership. My mother usually got her friend Bill to work on
it for a fifth of J&B whiskey. For that price he also bought all
the parts for the car from wrecking yards. From Bill I learned
how to flush a radiator and replace its hoses. I learned how to
replace spark plugs, adjust a carburetor, and replace a starter.
Bill had a sixth sense about mechanical things. He would lift
the hood, take a look, and almost immediately determine the
car's problem. Sometimes he just sniffed under the hood and
knew what was wrong.

Finally, after three summers the car broke down for the
last time and it was placed on blocks in the driveway.

I was the only one who still used it. I used to recline on
the long front bench, which accommodated the entire five-
foot, three-inch length of me. I often slept there in the sun,
which felt like napping in a warm bath. My mother played
goalie and stopped anyone who tried to disturb me while I
was resting or reading in Nellybelle.

I read everything I could get my hands on, and Nellybelle's
front seat was littered with books by Maya Angelou and
Stephen King, comic books, *True Romance* magazines, the
Herald Examiner, and copies of the *Los Angeles Sentinel*. One
summer I was determined to read the top ten fiction and
non-fiction books on the *New York Times* best sellers list.

My mother seemed to understand my appetite for *True Romance* magazines and Stephen King, but the rest of my reading material she couldn't get into. Her tastes were more of the Barbara Cartland variety—we had just about every romance novel ever published at our house, and my mother thought it outrageous when I told her that a story didn't always have to have a happy ending to be satisfying. I told her that she should read *Sophie's Choice*. She just wrinkled her nose and shook her head. She didn't want to read about people with such unhappy lives, she said.

When all of my friends were running to the mall that summer to flirt with boys or take in a movie, I was reclining in Nellybelle and reading until the light faded. Once or twice when I got to a good part, I went into the house to grab a flashlight, so I could finish a chapter before going inside for the night. Because of this I missed out on *Star Wars* and TV shows like *CHIPS*. The disco era completely passed me by in a blur of words on the page.

On particularly hot days I rolled down the windows and fanned myself with magazines. I couldn't be persuaded by my friends to leave my little Chevy library. And I especially liked it when my mother brought me lunch—a cool glass of milk and a banana and peanut butter sandwich.

We couldn't afford new books, so I would check them out from the library, or my mother would scour thrift shops at my request for used copies. She purchased *The Godfather* but refused to buy *The Exorcist*, telling me that it would give me nightmares. I secretly checked the book out from the library, and my mother was right about the nightmares.

At the end of that third summer, Nellybelle was sold for scrap, for fifty dollars. If I could have come up with the money to pay for Nellybelle myself, I would have, but we were about as broke as we'd ever been.

We needed the money, my mother said, because the welfare office had lost our monthly application, a peach-colored government form that came with carbon copies. People receiving welfare, however, weren't allowed to keep a copy. We had to send in the entire packet, and the welfare office would then mail our copy back to us. Questions on the form included, "Do you own a color TV?" and "Do you own a vehicle?" Such questions were asked, my mother told us, because we were not allowed to buy "luxury" items with government assistance.

Our cash assistance and our food stamps were put on hold for "ten working days," while they searched for our forms. There was nothing to be done. My mother said her nursing license had expired. We had no other income.

SEVEN

The Summer of the Fathers

Things were about as bad as they'd ever been when my mother decided to call in the fathers. Bobby called it the Summer of the Fathers, with Napoleon Boykin, father of the twins, Mark and Mariah; Willie Wright Sr., the father of Teresa and Little Willie; Morris Dolphin Sr., father of Morris; Edward Lee Hill, my father; Jesse Cotton, father of Bobby and Cynthia; and Roy Randolph, father of Yvonne and Steven.

I barely remembered most of the fathers. They paraded through our house in order of recent involvement. It probably would have been less confusing for the schools if we had all been given her last name and not those of our fathers. But my mother said "Then, you wouldn't be entitled to nothin', if one of those good-for-nothin' motherfuckahs ever made somethin' out of theyselves."

That summer, Napoleon (Nicky) Boykin decided to become involved in the twins' lives and took them to visit him and his new wife. Jesse Cotton—my least favorite stepfather—visited with Cynthia and Bobby but ignored the rest of us. One of my earliest memories was of Jesse Cotton blackening my mother's eye in a fistfight.

Years later I asked my mother what the fight had been about.

Jesse Cotton had come home from work one day, she said, and told her he'd gotten a second job so he could support his "other family" down the street.

"My mama told me not to marry that shit heel," she said of Jesse Cotton. "But I didn't listen. She said no redheaded fool that gambles and chases women would make me happy, and she was right."

When Jesse Cotton visited during the Summer of the Fathers, he had the same red hair and freckles that I remembered. I disliked freckles, especially on Black people. It looked like some kind of disease, I thought. But during the Summer of the Fathers, I noticed something else about Jesse Cotton. The left side of his face looked as if it were melting away, and he had a large hearing aid in his left ear.

"What happened to you?" I asked him.

"Ask yo' mama," he said.

My mother refused to tell me the story, so I asked Uncle Lo'.

"Yo' mama and Jesse sent they kids to stay with us for a few days, so they could talk about their relationship. You know they needed some grown-folk time together without a bunch of kids runnin' in and out," Uncle Lo' explained. "That weekend, Jesse Cotton had come home drunk and confessed that he had impregnated a neighbor lady. And yo' mama started in on him, and he threw her up against the kitchen table. The table damn near split in two, and she was knocked out cold. Yo' mama told us that Jesse was such a fool that he went to sleep in they bed after he had beat on her."

He continued, clearly enjoying this part of the story: "Now we was raised country and your mama knows a thing or two about how to get the hair off a hog."

My mother boiled a pot of water with lye in it, went into the bedroom, and dumped it over his head. She called an ambulance for him. The hospital staff must have called the police when they heard his story, but the police told Jesse that if he pressed charges for assault, my mother would too. Uncle Lo' said the cops just didn't want to do the paperwork, and besides, what did they care if Black people chose to mangle one another? When we'd returned home after that weekend at Uncle Lo's house, Jesse Cotton had fled. We did not see him again until the Summer of the Fathers.

During the Summer of the Fathers, Jesse Cotton gave Bobby and Cynthia fifty dollars between them. We didn't see him again for many years.

Roy Randolph showed up each weekend to take Steven and Yvonne to the swap meet to buy trinkets, mostly key chains. He usually had some woman, half his age, in the passenger seat of his car. He would introduce her by name and then say, "This is your new mother." He never seemed to tire of the joke. Roy kept promising Yvonne that he would buy her a car, if she got her high school diploma. He still didn't know that Yvonne couldn't read. As for Steven, he kept promising his son that he was going to take him to see a live wrestling match, if he graduated "regular" high school, and not "some program for dummies," as he put it. Steven graduated Locke High School in the regular program, but Roy Randolph never managed to take him to a wrestling match.

Big Willie kicked in the most by setting up a regular child support payment of eighty dollars a month for Teresa and Willie. The financial support would continue until they graduated high school, he said.

Morris's father was a sickly man and was at our house just long enough to say hello and give his son some money in secret. Morris refused to disclose how much.

My own father had not been seen for the better part of a decade, but somehow he was tracked down too. He was a tall man with dark, pockmarked skin. A dimple on his left cheek mirrored my own. His short black hair encircled a shiny bald spot. I noticed brown spots on his white dress shirt and his light-colored slacks. Both shirt and pants were fraying at the cuffs.

My mother told me to give him a hug.

"Why?" I said. "You said not to talk to strangers."

"I don't need no hug from her," he said, and parted the curtains to look out the window. "Can my girl come in?"

"You got yo' woman sittin' in a car on a hot day like this?" my mother said. "Tell her to get in here."

He left and then returned with a light-skinned woman in a short red halter dress. The cleavage went all the way down to her navel. She was pretty in a trampy sort of way and wore a lot of makeup. She stumbled as she crossed the doorway.

"Sit yo' drunk ass down, before you fall down," my mother said.

"Y'all got something to drink?" the woman slurred.

"Yeah, but I think you've had enough," my mother said, guiding the woman onto the black velvet couch. The woman sat down hard and it sounded like a baseball hitting a glove.

"I'm Mrs. Gordon and this here is Ed's daughter, Mary," my mother said by way of introduction.

For the first time, I noticed that my mother was using the honorific of Mrs., although Gordon was her maiden name. I guess she wanted Ed to think that she had someone too.

"High five," the woman said, and she held up her left hand. "I'm his wife, Monique."

I just rolled my eyes and sat across from her on the matching love seat. The woman's hand was still in the air. "Ahhh, y'all just gonna leave me hangin'?" she slurred.

My mother acted as if this happened every day of the week. She moved the woman's hand to a shaking position and shook it.

"Can I use yo' bathoon?" Monique said.

"Yeah," my mother said. "It's through the hall on the left."

Monique tried to rise but sank back down. Staying seated, she laughed at herself and slapped her bare thigh.

My mother shook her head and turned away. To my father she said, "You should give your daughter some money for her good grades. Mary, go get your report card."

But before I could rise to my feet, my father said, "I ain't givin' her no money. She got a smart mouth just like you."

"Okay, if you ain't gonna give her no money, at least buy the girl somethin' nice to show her that you proud of her," my mother said. "Her sister Cynthia got a bike. Why don't you buy Mary a bike?"

"I got a few dollars," he said, rising unsteadily. He stumbled over to me, and I could smell the liquor on his breath. He gave me three one-dollar bills, counting them out as if they were part of my inheritance.

"You still the cheapest-ass motherfuckah around," my mother said. "That's all you got for your chile after all this time?"

"Hey, you cain't talk to my man like that," Monique said as she managed to rise shakily from the sofa. She lurched in my mother's direction.

I thought the party was finally going to get started, but my mother just held up a warning hand and said, "Both y'all drunks can get the fuck out of my house."

That was it. They stumbled together out the door. I peeked through the curtains just in time to see Monique hike up her short dress. She was not wearing panties. She squatted and peed in the gutter in front of our house. Then they drove away with a squeal of tires on asphalt and a splash of urine.

I looked at the three dollars in my hand. Then I went into the kitchen and got some matches. Going out to the driveway, I placed the money in a stack on an oil spot where Nellybelle had once parked. I dropped a lighted match on the pile. The money didn't burn as well as it did in the movies, but the oil slick helped. By the time my mother emerged from the house and turned the water hose on the little conflagration, there was a good-sized hole in the bills where Washington's face should have been.

"Girl, you done lost yo' damn mind burning money," she said as she took the singed bills into the house. I stood in the driveway and stared at my distorted reflection in the oil slick.

I had been five years old the last time I had seen my father. We were all at Uncle Lo's house. He had one of those new hi-fi TV sets, and the whole neighborhood had turned out to watch an important broadcast. Somewhere in the crowd was my father. Uncle Lo' had scooped me up and presented me to him.

"Don't you wanna hold yo' baby?" he asked.

"Naw, holding kids puts my leg to sleep," he said. "I'ma get a beer."

He stumbled out of his seat and went into the kitchen.

Uncle Lo' shook his head and sat down, plopping me onto his lap. On the TV some guys in white baggy suits were coming down a ladder in what seemed like slow motion. One said something about making a leap for mankind.

"Look at those guys. They went all the way to the moon. I cain't hardly believe those crazy bastards really did it," Uncle Lo' said. "Say what you want about white boys, they know how to get shit done." I started to cry. "Don't waste yo' tears on some jive-ass nigga who cain't see what's right in front of him," Uncle Lo' told me.

Sticking my two favorite fingers in my mouth, I dozed off as Uncle Lo' rubbed my back.

My mother recalled me to the present when she came out of the house and stood behind me. She was not a woman given to public gestures of affection. But now she placed an arm over my shoulder.

"We can probably take the money to the bank," my mother said. "Somebody told me that as long as you still got half the bill, you can exchange it. When I get the new bills, you can keep the money if you want to."

What did she imagine? Did she think that I would frame it and hang it in my bedroom like some sort of shopkeeper who had earned his first dollar?

"Naw, you keep it, Ma," I said. "You need it more than me."

"He ain't worth no tears," my mother said. "You hear me?"

"Yeah, that's what they tell me," I sighed. Dry-eyed, I went into the house.

Eight

On the County

I was glad when the Summer of the Fathers was officially over. Most of the fathers stayed away after that. Only Big Willie and Roy Randolph showed up every weekend to take their kids to lunch.

The welfare office had found the forms, so we finally received our welfare check and food stamps. Shortly after that my mother went back to work part-time.

She told us that because her nursing license hadn't been renewed she could only find "mammy work," which involved scrubbing toilets and cleaning "up after nasty-ass white folks" in some downtown hotel. We still got partial government payments of food stamps and cash assistance, which was just enough to feed eight children.

I asked my mother why she didn't just renew her license, since she disliked "mammy work" so much, but she wouldn't answer. At the library I found reference books on the requirements for "timely" renewal for Licensed Vocational Nurses. One book stated that "licensees that renew their licenses prior to their expiration date, or within the thirty-day grace period for renewal are required to pay a fee of $100. The fee will be $200 thereafter."

When I told my mother this, she said, "Mind yo' own business, girl."

I thought I could get a part-time job mowing lawns or babysitting to earn money for my mother to renew her nursing license.

I imagined delivering two crisp $100 bills to my mother, and her hugging me and thanking me for believing in her. It was a nice feeling. I saved up every dollar from babysitting and started making lists of the lawns that needed mowing in the neighborhood.

Then one day I took out the old push mower from the shed as Uncle Lo' was coming up the walk.

"What you up to, gal? Mowin' is man's work. Where 'dem good-for-nothin' brothers of yours?"

"I'm gonna mow the neighbors' lawns and earn some money. I'm gonna help Mama get her nursing license back," I said proudly. "But don't tell her. It's a surprise."

"I see that Say ain't told you," he said, shaking his head. "That woman is so damn prideful. Come on the porch, girl, you should know about this."

The conversation with my Uncle Lo' went something like this:

"I told Sarah not to get involved with those damned Mexicans. I told her that they was gonna just drag her down," he said. "You know how your mother is. Anyway, they was paying a lot of the Mexican girls less at that convalescent hospital where yo' mama was workin'. Them girls told her that it was because they was illegal and they didn't have no papers. They told yo' mama they would give her Spanish lessons, if she helped them with the papers," he said. "So yo' mama puts on her jailhouse lawyer hat and starts teaching these heffas how to fill out them papers fo' citizenship. A few even got it, and then they started talking about unions and shit. And when the big boss said, 'Who is responsible for this mess?,' everybody pointed fingers at yo' mama, even them little heffas that she helped. So, yo' mama got fired. She probably ain't gonna be doin' that nursin' gig for a while."

I wanted to cry about the unfairness of it but I didn't. I never mentioned it again. I earned $100 that summer in babysitting and lawn-mowing money, and I gave it all to my mother. I told her to buy herself something nice.

My mother never went back to nursing. She had spent so much of her time learning it. She was one of the few

African Americans to graduate from Compton Community College in the 1950s with a degree in vocational nursing. She told me that her mother had been so proud of her because she was the first college graduate in the family for 100 years. My mother had kept her college degree in a little burgundy cardboard frame for many years. It was one of the casualties of the fire.

In the days that my mother was occupied with what she called "mammy work," we had frequent visits from the social workers, who wanted to make sure my mother wasn't earning enough money to go off welfare. We had to submit to spot inspections by the social worker, who went searching for luxury items. My mother locked her guns in a trunk, and, fortunately, every social worker seemed to accept the excuse that the key couldn't be found.

My mother owned a .45 automatic, a .22, a .38, a shotgun, and a rifle. She also possessed various daggers, knives, switchblades, and machetes.

I asked her once what all the firepower was for.

She said simply, "When the shit comes down one day, they is gonna protect theirs, and I'm gonna protect mine."

She did not elaborate. What shit? Where? Why? Who are they? I wanted to ask but I knew better. My mother loved the protection of her guns, but she didn't want to discuss it.

We didn't fire the guns very often. On New Year's Eve, with the rest of the neighborhood, we rang in the New Year by firing the guns into the air. The guns must be pointed straight up into the air, my mother told us. The only gun I wanted to fire was the .22 because it was small. I grasped it with both hands, aimed it above my head, and fired—pop, pop, pop—into the night sky. I didn't like the burned-match smell, but it didn't make my ears ring or blow me back on my ass like the shotgun used to.

Cynthia always fired the .22 pistol with toilet paper stuffed in her ears. She was always trying to prove that she was more delicate than the rest of us. I thought the toilet paper was stupid and just for show. You could still hear everything. Besides, what was the point of firing a gun if you didn't hear the shots? The noise was part of the celebration, I thought.

I wondered what the social workers would have thought if they had known that my mother had enough guns in her trunk to arm most of our family. They breezed through our house about once a month. We stood by quietly while they went through our stuff. My mother just sat at the kitchen table, rolling cigarettes and staring into her cold coffee.

Cynthia said the social workers just needed to check boxes on their forms. They didn't mean any harm. And I don't think any of them enjoyed going through people's drawers and cabinets. I asked a social worker once what she was looking for. She told me that she wanted to see if we were hiding a color TV set or if there was men's clothing in the closet. No men were allowed to live in the house under their rules.

We had an old 19-inch black-and-white TV set that you had to turn on and off with a pair of pliers because the knob had broken off. That television did not produce sound. Placed on top of the 19-inch TV, we had another 13-inch black-and-white TV that had sound but no picture. If we had them on the same channel at the same time, the two TVs worked as one.

The big TV was a hand-me-down from Uncle Lo'. He couldn't locate the rabbit ears—that spiffy television antenna that had those two rods in a nice V shape. So, we just used a coat hanger sticking out of the back. Channel 2 was the only station that came in clearly. Fortunately for me, it was CBS, which showed *The Carol Burnett Show* and *The Sonny and Cher Comedy Hour*, which were my favorites.

As far as the men's clothing was concerned, the social worker told me that there was a "man in the house" rule. Under this rule, a child was denied welfare benefits if the child's mother was living, or having relations, with any able-bodied male. I almost blurted out that there were plenty of men around, but they didn't keep their clothes at our house. But I clamped my mouth shut when I remembered what my mother had said about putting the household business in the street.

Sometimes the social workers would try to help. They told my mother that because she worked part-time our food stamp payments were going to be cut but she could get a voucher for some "government cheese." The "gubment cheese shit," as Bobby called it, was a large orange block of cheese about the size of a brick and just as hard. Once you pried a piece loose with the help of a butter knife and a hammer, it tasted something like cheese and smelled like old musty clothes left in the bottom of the hamper too long. Worst of all, you had to go downtown to a charity office to pick it up. I didn't like standing in the "gubment cheese-shit" line. I was afraid that someone from school would see me. I told my mother so.

"And I want you always to remember something here, gal," my mother said. "There ain't no shame in bein' poor. Jesus was not a rich man, and he was the greatest man who ever lived. Think about Jesus and how he ministered to the poor. In 1 Timothy 6 it say, 'We have brought nothing into the world, and neither can we carry anything out. So, having sustenance and covering, we shall be content with these things.'"

Sometimes my mother knew exactly the right thing to say and when to say it. I stood proudly next to her in the "gubment cheese-shit" line, and I thought of it as the fulfillment of prophecy.

Sometimes during the lean times when there wasn't even "gubment cheese shit" to eat, my mother would go hunting for our dinner. A new low-income housing project was being built in our neighborhood, and my mother said she'd seen plenty of rabbits in the field near the construction site. I remembered the first time she loaded up her .22 rifle for the hunt and went out to the field.

We were city children and very embarrassed about my mother hunting for rabbits in a nearby field. We heard the shots, and pretty soon she came in with a couple of dead cottontails.

"I'ma get some vegetables from the garden and we gonna have rabbit stew tonight," my mother said, proudly tossing the rabbits onto the kitchen counter.

"I ain't eatin' that," Bobby said.

"Me neither," I agreed.

"Then go hungry," my mother said. "I ain't no short-order cook up in this motherfuckah. You cain't just have it your way," she said, paraphrasing the latest Burger King commercial. "I don't know how I done raised such pansy-ass brats," she added.

My mother borrowed a few potatoes from our neighbor and pulled up some onions, carrots, and squash from her garden. Then she skinned and gutted the rabbits. She put the pot on in the morning and didn't take it off the heat until early evening. The whole house smelled like roasted meat and stew. We hadn't eaten in two full days. Our stomachs were competing for which had the loudest growl. My mother sat at the table blowing on her stew. My siblings and I watched her from the hallway, crowded into the narrow space like puppies waiting to nurse.

"You stupid-ass kids better get some bowls before I eat all this," she said without turning around.

She didn't have to ask us twice. We practically climbed over one another to get into the pot. We devoured the stew with gusto and dutifully forgot how it had been obtained.

Nine

Going Down South

The rabbit stew reminded me of a previous time we had seen an animal killed to feed us when we went to visit my mother's relatives in Alexandria, Louisiana.

During the trip—I was about nine at the time—it seemed to me that our family was caught perpetually in a game of City Mouse versus Country Mouse. We were visiting our great-grandmother on my mother's side, who lived in a cabin without running water or electricity. We had to pump water from a well. The bathroom was an outhouse. Everything was cooked on a wood-burning pot-bellied stove and the place was lit at night by kerosene lamps that cast strange shadows on the floor, which seemed to wiggle and shiver in the dark like living things.

My great-grandmother was in her eighties, but she still rode her bicycle ten miles roundtrip every day to get fresh milk and butter from the nearest store. She grew most of her own vegetables in a dirt lot behind her shack and kept a few chickens.

During one visit, she asked Bobby and Steven—who were fifteen and nineteen, respectively—to chop wood so she could make the evening meal. Finally, when my brothers had been at it for over an hour with no results, she came out of the house.

"What is wrong with you boys?" she said. "I gotta get the pots on for supper. We gotta get these babies' bellies full. Babies sleep real good with full bellies."

"Big Mama, we don't know how to do it," Steven admitted.

"Gimme dat," she said, grabbing the axe and shoving the two teenagers out of the way. She spat once on each wrinkled and gnarled hand, then proceeded to split the wood. Crack! Crack! Crack! The axe made a sound like a bat hitting a home run.

"Y'all 'Fonia folk don't know your ass from a hole in the ground," she said, pointing at the wood. My brothers picked it up and carried it into her shack.

Later that same week we went to visit my mother's aunt Frozine. "What is 'Fonia folk'?" I asked her.

"That's what they call you 'round here," Aint Frozine said. "Y'all from 'Fonia, ain't ya?"

I stared at my mother, who responded, "They mean California."

"Dat's what I say," Aint Frozine said. "Don't need no translator."

My mother's aunt lived in a large modern house with the plumbing indoors where it belonged, but she still worshipped at the church of fresh meat and produce.

Cynthia and I were playing jump rope in her backyard, when we were called to attention. "Y'all need to go out to the henhouse, grab a couple of those chickens, and dress 'em for dinner," Aint Frozine yelled.

Cynthia and I exchanged a look.

"What do you mean?" Cynthia asked. "Yo' chickens wear dresses?"

We both laughed at the thought of it.

"Y'all need to go get a couple of the hens and dress 'em for dinner," Aint Frozine repeated, but this time very slowly, as if we were slow in our understanding of things.

When we didn't move, she stared at us and huffed.

"Y'all gotta kill 'em, pluck 'em, and fry 'em up," she said. "What is y'all, 'bout ten and thirteen? I know yo' mammy den taught you how ta do this."

"We get our chickens wrapped in plastic at the supermarket," I chimed in. "Why don't you do that?"

Aint Frozine slammed the back door behind her as she disappeared into the house. Score one for the city mouse, I thought.

Cynthia and I went back to jumping rope and singing.

Aunt Frozine emerged from the back door carrying a hatchet. The red roses on her housedress seemed to grow with each step. I blinked, tripped over the jump rope, and fell on my face. I tasted dirt and blood.

Aint Frozine's large calloused hand yanked me up by the collar. I was propelled on my tiptoes toward the chicken coop, Cynthia following close behind. My great-aunt shoved me down in the dirt next to the chicken house and then grabbed Cynthia by the collar and deposited her next to me. In the chicken coop the birds were in a panic, making kuh-kuh-kuh-kack sounds.

Cynthia and I exchanged panicky looks as Aint Frozine exited the coop with a squawking, thrashing chicken gripped in one hand and the hatchet in her other.

She placed the bird on the chopping block, and thwack, its head came off. It seemed as though the body was still alive and wanted to run around without its head. On the stump the beak opened and closed just once. Aint Frozine grabbed the body by its feet and let the blood drop onto the dirt yard. I covered my eyes and Cynthia threw up.

I smelled blood and the distinct odor of peppermint Fixodent as Aint Frozine got down next to my ear. "And dat's how ya gets chickens," she whispered.

The country mouse takes the lead, I thought.

When my mother came to pick us up, we told her breathlessly about the chicken slaughter.

"Yeah, that sound like Frozine," my mother said. "She always was country. And she ain't got patience for people who ain't. And you know she believe that kids should be seen and not heard," she said, looking directly at me. "When is you gonna learn that if you ain't flappin' your gums, you might just learn something?"

My mother was very proud of her country roots, but she didn't want to return to the South to live.

"Too many honkies who think they shit don't stink," she said.

On another of our trips to see the Louisiana relatives, we stopped at a gas station, back in those days when a guy would run out and fill the tank up. A big-bellied white man in coveralls with no shirt came out of the station, saw our color, and looked as though he'd rather not have our business.

"Fill her up with ethyl," my mother told him, looking him directly in the eyes. "And I'd like a pack of Virginia Slims."

The white man hesitated, but he began filling the car up. Then the man went into the station, and we had a long wait before he came out with a pack of Winston cigarettes and tossed them through the car window at my mother. Meanwhile, Big Willie sat in the driver's seat, as still as the hot southern air. He must have been angry but he didn't show it, knowing what could happen if we made trouble. But my mother wasn't about to put up with this kind of treatment and it didn't matter that we were in a part of the country where white people typically treated Blacks as inferiors.

My mother looked at the pack, and then she looked at the pump.

"Look here, Mr. Motherfuckah, them ain't Virginia Slims and that ain't ethyl," she said. "You don't just gimme what you feel like and expect to be paid for it."

The man screwed up his nose and walked to the rear of the car, glancing at our plate.

"Oh, y'all from 'Fonia," he said. "Y'all ain't familiar at how we do things 'round here."

Big Willie gripped the steering wheel tightly, saying nothing.

"I know how you crazy-ass white folks do," my mother said. "I grew up not ten miles down this here road."

Finally, Big Willie unfurled his fists from the steering wheel and handed the man twenty dollars.

"We gotta get down the road 'fo dark," Big Willie said. "We is expected."

The man looked at the money, took it, pulled an oil-stained rag from his back pocket, and wiped the back of his neck. He didn't say anything more. And he didn't offer any change.

My mother folded her arms across her chest and sat back in the passenger seat. Big Willie drove out of the driveway with squealing tires.

"What da' hell, Willie," my mother said. "That pecker-wood disrespected me and didn't bring you yo' change."

"I know, Sarah, but we got the babies in the car," he said, turning to look at six of us huddled in the back seat. "Won't do no good to get in trouble down here. You been up north too long and forgot how crazy them white fools can be down here. They been done kilt everybody in the car just 'cause you don't like the cigarettes and the gas he give ya."

My mother tapped two Winstons out of the package, put them both in her mouth, and lit them. She gently placed one of the cigarettes between Big Willie's parted lips. He smoked it down to the butt without taking his hands off the steering wheel.

It seemed to me that my mother didn't like the South much or her Southern relatives.

"Why do we spend every other summer in Louisiana?" I asked her.

"They is some nice things down there," she said. "Everybody ain't in such a big hurry. You learn that you don't need to break your neck to get from here to there. If you wait, sometimes stuff comes to you. And you learn some stuff about standin' on your own." And my mother's final lesson about the South: "And when you go down home, you come back and appreciate what you got."

The entire family seemed relieved when we got back to California. We rolled out of the car as if we'd just been released from prison. We were glad to be back where we had indoor plumbing, electric lights, and a gas stove.

TEN

Closer to Home

Soon enough, like a sobered-up drunk who forgets the hangover, we were taking everything for granted again. We left the TV tuned to its one channel, whether we were in the room or not, and we ran full baths for our baby dolls.

I particularly didn't like the trips down South, not just because I was a child hell-bent on being seen and heard, but because I had to sit next to Cynthia in the car. We fought constantly. And I don't mean white girl-style screaming matches like Kristy McNichol used to do on TV's *Family*, but I mean knock-down-drag-out fistfights. We rested in opposite corners of the living room between such bouts, like two fighters waiting for word from the corner man to resume our slug match.

Long car trips were difficult because we couldn't go to opposite ends of the living room. A person sitting in the back seat with you is still within striking distance, even if four other people are sandwiched between you.

Cynthia, being two years older, always tried to assert her big-sister authority over me. Our fights increased when we finally got a TV that displayed channels two through thirteen. I was watching *Mutual of Omaha's Wild Kingdom* on Channel 4, and she switched it to *The Wizard of Oz* on Channel 7.

"Hey, I was watching that!" I protested.

"I don't care," Cynthia said. "Everybody wants to see *The Wizard of Oz* and you're the only one who wants to see that animal crap."

Of course, I turned the TV back to my channel. She turned it to Channel 7, and I turned it back. We went on like that for several minutes until the knob snapped off in my hand.

"You stupid heffa," she said. "Mama gonna kill you for breakin' that."

"Hey, you is the one that broke it!" I yelled.

Cynthia slapped my face, and the next thing you know we were rolling on the floor, trying to mangle each other. Yvonne broke up the fight. When my mother got home from work, we were both in trouble. My mother never wanted to hear about who started the fight. The house rule was that brothers and sisters should never raise their hands to each other.

"You gonna get enough fightin' in the streets, and you don't have to come home to it," my mother would say.

The "No fighting" rule was not written down anyplace, but we all knew it. And if we violated it, there was always a whuppin' coming our way.

"You two crazy heffas den broke the new TV, and you been fightin'," my mother said. "Go get some switches."

Choosing your own switch was an art form. You didn't want it so big that the branch would break the skin, but you didn't want it too small either because then Mama would go get the biggest limb on the tree and give you a lashing you would never forget. I chose a medium branch, put on some shorts, and waited for Cynthia to do the same. Switching was always done right below the knee. I could see the distress in my mother's face as each blow fell.

"What did I tell you about fightin' up in this house," my mother said, and that was worth eleven lashes on the legs. Each word was a lash. I closed my eyes and could hear the switch go back like a wasp flying too close to the ear.

Cynthia got the same. I could hear her crying before the switch even touched her legs. I started crying about halfway in.

"Stop cryin'," my mother commanded, after the whuppin'. "Now hug your sister."

This was the worst part of the whole affair. I really didn't like Cynthia, and I would have taken another eleven lashes just to skip the hug, but I hugged her anyway. I just wanted it to be over with, so I could just put some cream on my welts and go to bed.

As we grew older, Cynthia and I fought even more. We shared a bedroom, which didn't help matters On my side of the room I had posters of the latest Black celebrities, like Kevin Hooks, Philip Michael Thomas, the Jackson Five, George Benson, and my favorite, Billy Dee Williams.

Cynthia's side of the room featured white rock groups like the Bay City Rollers, Peter Frampton, Leif Garrett, and KISS. Bobby often joked that we lived in the most segregated house in the neighborhood.

I came home from a difficult day at junior high school to find tape over Billy Dee Williams's eyes. "What in the hell is this?" I asked Cynthia.

"I just felt like his eyes was on me when I'm getting dressed," she said.

"Yeah, lucky you," I said. "I'm gonna take this tape off and if it tears my poster I'm gonna kick your black ass."

"Bring it on," she said.

As I carefully removed the tape from Billy Dee's eyes, his left eye started to peel off on the tape. I screamed and grabbed Cynthia across the collar, pitching her over the bed. She leaped on me and the fight was on.

I quickly grew tired of these battles with Cynthia, but she had no off-switch. After we'd each gotten in one or two good punches I was ready to call it quits, but Cynthia was the Energizer Bunny of fistfights. She would not stop fighting once she got going.

Bobby told me that when I'd had enough, I should put Cynthia in a wrestling hold until she calmed down. He showed me how to do a few. So, with Bobby's help, I became adept at chinlocks, half- and full-Nelsons, and reverse cradles. But there was always plenty of slugging before I could successfully maneuver Cynthia into a wrestling-hold position.

Another point of friction between Cynthia and me was that my mother dressed us in matching clothing until I was eight and Cynthia was ten. My mother made all of our clothes on her old Singer sewing machine that she'd inherited from her mother. She would purchase one large discount bolt of cloth and make two identical dresses with it. The problem was that Cynthia was a tomboy, and she was big on climbing fences, trees, or just about anything, really. Her dresses would wind up with a number of holes and rips, and then she would start wearing mine. My mother also bought us underwear with the days of the week marked on them. I usually got Monday, Wednesday, and Friday, while Cynthia got Tuesday, Thursday, and Saturday. Sunday was up for grabs. Cynthia invariably got it.

Our arguments would usually go something like this:

"You better not be wearing my dress and my Monday panties," I would say.

"So what if I am?" Cynthia taunted. "You cain't do nothing about it."

At bath time I would notice that Cynthia was indeed wearing Monday, so I decided to tear them off her. And so we were fighting, again. These battles only started to taper off when I returned from summer camp.

In the year before I began junior high school, I got the opportunity to go away to camp. My teacher, Mrs. Warren, believed that inner-city children should have the opportunity to go to summer camp. She worked out an agreement with local businesses to sponsor five children from Figueroa Elementary School to attend Camp Brea in the Santa Monica Mountains.

"We're going to give a summer-camp scholarship to several of our top scholars," she announced one morning after the Pledge of Allegiance.

I was standing dutifully in the back of the classroom and

not reciting the pledge, as usual, but I could have sworn that Mrs. Warren had looked directly at me when she said this.

Later that week a special school assembly was held to announce the school's top five students. I received a certificate upon which was written: Awarded to Mary Hill on this fifth day of May in the Year of Our Lord Nineteen Hundred and Seventy Sixth, a scholarship to attend Camp Brea.

Eleven

Away From the Family

I stared at the certificate, half expecting it to disappear, tracing my fingers over the raised gold letters. I slipped it inside one of my textbooks and skipped all the way home, the book clasped to my chest.

"Mama, Mama!" I burst in the door breathless, brandishing my certificate. "I got a scholarship!"

My mother glanced over my certificate. Her brows rose, and she pursed her lips forward. Uh-oh, I thought. This can't be good.

"Camp is for white folks," she said, handing me back my certificate.

"No, no," I insisted. "Mrs. Warren said that she put up only the best students for camp. She said we can go horseback riding, swimming, and play tennis, and everything."

"You cain't swim, and you cain't ride a horse or play tennis," my mother said.

"They can teach me," I said.

"You don't need to be away for a whole summer to learn that stuff," my mother said. "You ain't goin' to no camp."

My eyes filled with tears.

"Don't be cryin' over no bullshit," my mother said. "Or I'm gonna give ya somethin' to cry about."

I walked very slowly to school the next day and kept my head down as I entered the classroom. I placed the camp certificate on Mrs. Warren's desk. She looked over her cateye glasses at me, the same glasses that my mother wore. But other than their glasses, the two women couldn't have been more different in appearance. Mrs. Warren was tall, thin, and very light skinned. That day she wore one of her beautiful, quilted satin dresses in alternating colors of blue, red, and green with brown suede lace-up boots. Her hair was pulled into two ball-shaped puffs that stuck out on either side of her head, with a part down the middle that revealed her gleaming pink scalp. Her hairstyle was just about the only thing that reminded you that she was Black.

"You're late," she said. "We need to meet at recess."

At recess, I told her about my mother's objections to summer camp. She gave me a sealed note to take to my mother. I didn't open the note, but I was not surprised when Mrs. Warren came to our house on Saturday.

Stepping gracefully, she came up our walk, wearing a red, white, and blue checkerboard print dress and matching pants. Her platform shoes made her look even taller. She was like a queen coming to visit.

I was sent out of the room, but I stood in the hallway, just out of my mother's sight. I was able to hear everything. Mrs. Warren, facing the hallway, could see me.

"Thank you for seeing me, Mrs. Gordon," my teacher said. "As I said in my note, I wanted to talk about Mary's scholarship and her opportunity to attend camp."

"She ain't got no suitcase," my mother said.

"She can borrow one of mine," Mrs. Warren said. "I just got a matching set for Christmas. I'm sure I can spare one."

"I don't want her going in no water and drowning, or getting thrown from some horse and winding up in a wheelchair," my mother said. "You know kids, once they get out of your sight, they do whatever they want. They can get kilt if you ain't on 'em twenty-four-seven."

"You know, Mrs. Gordon, I watch Mary every day, and she never says the Pledge of Allegiance with the other kids," Mrs. Warren said. "And she gets some heat because of it too. But you said no, so it's no."

Just then, Mrs. Warren did something that I thought strange. She looked at me and she winked. She moved her chair closer to my mother's, placed a hand on her arm, and she whispered something in her ear. She went on whispering for quite a while, and my mother nodded a couple of times.

Just before school the following day, my mother told me I could go to camp over the summer. This time I didn't slouch to school, I ran. I was early. Mrs. Warren was already in the classroom.

"What did you say to my mama?" I asked breathlessly. "I'm going to summer camp!"

"Well, you told me that your mother was a Witness or studying with them, right?" I nodded. "I told her that camp would be a good time to bear witness to others," Mrs. Warren said. "My aunt was a Witness and she was big on witnessing by example. I told your mother that it would be a great witness for rich people to see you there, and not giving in to pressures to do things that she didn't want you to do, just like when you stand in the back of the classroom when we do the Pledge. I told her you were a good example of Exodus 20:12, where it says to honor your parents."

Why, I didn't think of that, I thought. My mother hardly ever listened to any authority except the Bible.

Mrs. Warren handed me the scholarship paper and told me that she would deliver the suitcase to my house over the weekend. She also gave me a list of items that I would need for camp.

I frowned at the list. It included:

1. emergency whistle
2. life jacket
3. flashlight
4. hiking boots
5. envelopes
6. stamps
7. paper
8. pens and pencils
9. sleeping bag
10. swimming togs

"I can probably get a few of these—" I began.

"I can put one or two things in the suitcase that you might need," Mrs. Warren said with a smile.

I noticed she had drawn a line through number ten, which was a relief because I wasn't quite sure what a tog included.

"Now don't make a fool out of me, Miss Hill," she said. I liked her calling me that. It made me feel grown up and responsible. "Remember to honor your mother and follow her rules and the camp's rules when you get there. This is a big opportunity for you and for the school. I didn't just tell your mother all that stuff about you so she would let you go. I happen to believe it."

I nodded, impressed and pleased that she had such a good opinion of me.

"I see courage in you, Miss Hill," she said. "The kind that will take our people into the next century, and I want other people to see it too."

I had always liked Mrs. Warren. She seemed different than the other teachers. On the first day of sixth grade, we were all told on the public address system to rise for the Pledge of Allegiance. I walked to the back of the classroom, where I stood silently amid curious stares and laughter to stand.

One girl in the back row whispered to the boy next to her, "She is so weird. She did the same thing last year."

And just when the class had gotten to "one nation under God," Mrs. Warren approached me. She held her right hand over her heart and was reciting the pledge. She stood beside me as I held my breath, placing her left hand on my shoulder. The Pledge complete, I exhaled. Hand still on my shoulder, Mrs. Warren escorted me to my seat. She took her place in front of the classroom and began the lesson. No big deal, her actions seem to be saying. Nothing to see here, folks. Just go back to your work.

On the day I left for camp, my mother walked me to the bus stop.

We did not speak for the entire three-mile trek. When the

bus arrived, I threw my arms around her, but she didn't return the hug. I scrambled aboard the bus and rushed to the
large rear window to see if my mother was waving goodbye.
I could only see her back as she was walking away. She never
turned around.

I wrote a letter home every day and mailed them with the
stamps that Mrs. Warren had put in the suitcase for me. I
received one letter from my mother. She hoped I was having
a good time, and she told me to be good, and to mind the
counselors. She signed it, Your mother, Sarah Gordon.

Camp was very organized. Each day we kept to a schedule
of arts, crafts, hiking, and sports. I learned to play tennis but
not well, having never held a racquet before. I didn't quite
understand why you weren't supposed to hit the ball over
the fence. But I was the star of the girl's kickball team. One
girl said I kicked like a mule. In crafts, I made a clay ashtray,
five key chains, a puka shell necklace, and a basket. I was determined to have gifts for everyone when I got home. In the
evening we had campfires and ghost stories and a wonderful
treat that the white kids called S'mores.

For the first time, I came into contact with white children.
We all seemed to have a crush on David Cassidy and Foster
Sylvers, and we were all dreamy-eyed over the prospect of
our first kiss. The bunk beds we slept in were exactly like
the ones that Cynthia and I shared at home. They weren't
really so different from me, I realized. They were just light-
er-skinned.

On Sundays a few of the girls went to chapel. A counselor
told me that I had a written excuse and was not required
to attend. On those days I, along with a few of the other
non-churchgoers, would go on nature walks with an un-
churched camp counselor. On one such evening hike, I had
just taken out Mrs. Warren's loaned flashlight, when an owl
swooped down and made off with a screeching rat. *Mutual
of Omaha's Wild Kingdom* ain't got nothin' on camp, I thought.
Later that night we attended a talk on reptiles.

We peered at a glass aquarium as the counselor fed a mouse to a yellow rat snake. Many of the girls in the group cried. I did not. It was like seeing *Wild Kingdom* live. I didn't watch that show to see cute animals nursing their young. I loved it when Marlin Perkins's smooth, calm voice would describe a lion stalking and eating a zebra or anything else that wasn't fast enough to get away. There was something about the orderliness of nature that I found comforting, where chicken did not come wrapped in plastic from the supermarket. All creatures had to eat, and sometimes it got messy.

When summer camp was done, the yellow bus dropped us off at school after dark. We had been gone a long time in kid days. There were many tearful greetings as parents swept up their children. But I didn't see my mother. I knew it was too soon to panic, but I started to get worried as the parking lot began to look increasingly deserted.

Finally, I saw Bobby running toward me.

"Where's Mama?" I wanted to know.

"She cain't come and get you because she is sick," Bobby said. "And before you ask me a billion questions, it's her regular stuff when she gets those bad headaches and goes to bed for a day or two. Yvonne's come over, and she's doing all the cooking and cleaning. I'm in charge of transport, protection, and general maintenance. Same old, same old. She didn't want you ta get attacked or nothin' so she sent me."

"You're my bodyguard?" I asked, in a mocking tone that only a little sister could master.

"I told her that ain't nobody want to attack nothin' like you no way. And if they did take you, somebody would have to pay us to take you back," Bobby said, and then tried to give me a boot in the rear.

"Whatever," I said, skipping out of the way of the blow.

Bobby carried my suitcase. I had to admit I did feel a bit safer with my big brother next to me. Bobby was as wide as a refrigerator and lifted weights on our porch every day. If I squinted, I could see a resemblance to Mr. Poitier. Bobby's dark complexion made his teeth glow white like Chiclets gum in the moonlight. His front teeth were slightly darker than the rest because they'd been replaced after the originals were knocked out in a fight. He was just sixteen but his hair was already beginning to thin on the sides.

Our neighbors called him Crazy Bob because he'd once taken on three bullies with a baseball bat. Two were admitted to hospital and the other we never saw in our neighborhood again. After that, people crossed the street when they saw Bobby coming. Once, when I was in third grade, five girls chased me because I had reminded our teacher to pick up the homework. Bobby saw them chasing me. He grabbed me, sat me down on a curb, and went over to the girls. Bobby got the girls to huddle up like they were in a football game. I was wheezing and breathing so loud that I couldn't hear them although they were just a few feet away.

The girls told me later that Bobby had said, "See that little girl over there? If you mess with her, I'm going to gut you like a fish, and then I'm going to sneak into your house at night and gut your parents." The last part they told me in a whisper.

I told my mother about it and Bobby got a whuppin' with an extension cord. Then my mother called each of the girls' parents and apologized and swore to them that Bobby would not harm them. Just the same, the girls kept their distance from me at school. Bobby asked me if I'd told my mother what had happened, and I confessed that I had. I thought he'd pound me, but he just said, "Just let me know if those girls bother you again."

Now, as I walked home from the parking lot with Bobby beside me some years later, I said, "You remember that time those girls were chasing me?"

"Yeah," he said.

"I'm sorry I got you in trouble," I said.

"Just took one for the team, that's all," he said simply.

I don't think I could have loved him any more than I did

at that moment. I tried to take his hand. "Let's not get all sloppy lovey-dovey about it," he said and tried to use my hand to blow his nose.

I giggled and snatched my hand away.

Twelve

A Witness Phase

There was a lot of cool stuff at camp, Bobby," I told him. "You should have been there. Wait until I tell you what I saw—"

"Yeah, before you go off on one of your motormouth tours, there's something you should know that's going on at home," he said. "Mama is in a Witness phase and you know what that means?"

I stopped, saluted, and recited the list: "No smoking, no bad movies, no bad TV, no bad books, prayer of thanks before every meal, public and private, prayer before bed, and no pagan holidays, which means all holidays up to and including birthdays."

"You don't smoke so that's no big deal for you, but you're forgetting the most important one," he said.

I searched my memory. It had been a few years since the last Witness phase.

Then, saluting again, I replied in my most soldier-like voice, "Yes, sir! Bible study every Saturday in the living room, and Sunday is Kingdom Hall for every kid under twelve. Sir!"

I did an exaggerated march in place while saluting.

"Mama probably won't make you go to the Hall if you really don't want to," Bobby said, laughing.

"Hey, I happen to like the Kingdom Hall," I said. "Everything is organized, on time, and always clean, just like camp. And people ain't constantly telling you to leave the room because they're supposedly talking about stuff you cain't understand."

"You are one twisted sister," Bobby said.

"We moved since the last phase, so how did the Witnesses find us this time? Do you think it could have been my teacher who sent the Witnesses over?" I inquired. "She did say someone in her family was one of Jehovah's Witnesses or something."

"Could be, but it don't make no difference," Bobby said. "Mama is the only person in the city who always lets them in. She cain't get over the fact that her mother was one," he said. "Now march, soldier! Hup, two, three, four," Bobby ordered in his drill sergeant voice. We marched in lockstep, stopping only when the house came into view. My mother wouldn't have appreciated the joke.

Our house was a yellow stucco bungalow with an attached garage, just big enough for half a car. My mother said it was built for storage and not a vehicle. It was probably just as well that we didn't own a car, I thought.

Someone had painted the aluminum door a bright neon green. The paint was chipping in spots, revealing a dirty silver color beneath. One of my cousins, playing Evel Knievel one summer, had run his bike into the garage on a dare. He was fine but the door had hung oddly ever since, like a man hit in the stomach and forever crumpled over the blow. Cynthia mowed the lawn twice a week. The yard had bald spots but was no better or worse than any other lawn in the neighborhood.

Inside there were three bedrooms for the nine of us. My mother shared a room with the twins, Mark and Mariah. Willie, Morris, Bobby, and Steven were in the "boys' room." Cynthia and I had bunk beds in the "girls' room," which until recently we had shared with Yvonne, who had taken her king-size bed with her when she moved out.

The biggest problem was that there was only one bathroom. If someone got to the toilet ahead of you and you couldn't wait, then you had to pee in the tub and wash it out. If you had to do some other business, then you were expected to get it done in a bucket and dump it in the toilet later.

When I got home, no one seemed to want to hear about camp. Everyone sat in front of the TV, eating their pinto-beans-and-rice dinner, watching an episode of *Sanford and Son.*

"We been waiting all week for this new episode," Cynthia said, when I tried to hand her the puka shell necklace that I had made for her. "You can tell us about that stupid camp tomorrow."

"Whatever," I said, placing the necklace back in the suitcase.

My mother offered me some dinner, but I told her that we'd eaten dinner at camp before getting on the bus. She made a big deal about the clay ashtray I'd made for her. She'd given up smoking, but she was sure she could use it as a coaster.

The next day was Saturday—Bible study day. Usually we slept until ten on Saturdays and watched *Creature Feature* before going out to play. But during the Witness phase, we were all expected to take seats in the living room by nine and wait quietly for the study to begin.

There was a knock at the door and I opened it. Standing before me was a very wide, light-skinned Black woman in a dark blue dress with a white bib. She filled the doorway and sported the shadow of a mustache on her upper lip. Her long brown hair was pulled back in a ponytail. I could see white support hose in the four-inch space between the hem of her dress and her ankle. She wore black penny loafers without the pennies and had a cloth messenger bag hanging over her left hip.

"Oh, you're the one I haven't met yet," she said in a deep voice. "You must be Mary."

I nodded yes, and she bent down to meet my eyes. "How was camp?" she asked.

"Fine," I said, opening the door to let her in.

"I have a book for you," she said, and handed me a copy of *The Truth that Leads to Eternal Life.* It was ocean blue, and it had an etching of what looked like a book throwing off light monogrammed on the cover.

I was about to tell her that we had read the book several times already in previous Bible studies, when she asked: "Do you know God's name?"

"I don't even know your name," I said.

"Oh, silly me," she said. "I'm Sister Thomas."

"Your first name is Sister?" I asked pertly.

"Of course not," she said seriously. "Is your mother home?"

"Ma! Sister Thomas is here," I yelled.

My mother emerged from the bedroom.

Everyone else was already present and starting to find seats. I sat on a milk crate near my mother's chair. I had missed her over the summer.

"Sister Gordon, I was thinking that you could do the prayer today like we discussed last time."

My mother removed a note from her house-dress pocket. We all bowed our heads at the same time.

"Jehovah, our most kind and heavenly father," my mother began, "once again we approach your mighty throne of un-derserved kindness to study your word, the Bible. For where two or more are gathered together in your name, you are present also. It is with your guidance we now approach your heavenly words to write them upon our hearts and minds so we can endure all things until the end comes. We pray for sisters and brothers in all lands. In Jesus's name, Amen."

During Bible study, everyone got a chance to read and look up scriptures. Everyone had their own personal copy of the *Truth* book and *The New World Translation of the Holy Scriptures*.

When it was Yvonne's turn to read, she suddenly got a coughing or sneezing fit and left the room. She still couldn't read beyond a fourth-grade level, even though the rest of us pretended she could.

Steven could read well, but the words came out sounding

like he had a swollen tongue. I had been reading the Bible aloud since I was four years old, so it was no big deal for me. Cynthia read so quietly that Sister Thomas often asked her to read again. I rolled my eyes, thinking that there she was pretending to be more delicate than the rest of us, again. Mark and Mariah, being toddlers, were excused from reading, but they were expected to recite the names of the Apostles.

Morris squirmed in his seat because he wanted to watch *Creature Feature* or *Twilight Zone* instead of studying some "musty old Bible," he said. Little Willie preferred to do something more physical with his weekends. He was the best climber in the neighborhood and could use his hands and bare feet to scale any tree, including palms. Sometimes the neighborhood kids would pay him ten cents just to watch him scamper up a tree like a Capuchin monkey from *Wild Kingdom.*

When it was his turn, Bobby read everything like a Sunday radio preacher, exaggerating the scriptures until they sounded comical.

"'For with the heart one exercises faith for righteousness, but with the mouth one makes public declaration for salvation,' and that's Romans 10:10," Bobby shouted. "Oh! Glory! Can the congregation get an Amen?"

Sister Thomas rolled her eyes and simply turned to the next chapter in the *Truth* book. My mother glared at Bobby. "Boy, don't you be disrespectful before God," my mother said, interrupting the reading. "You know what happened to Goliath when he didn't show the proper respect to God's people."

In a previous Bible study, we had been taught that David had killed Goliath with a slingshot and then beheaded him in a "righteous killing" because the giant had spoken disrespectfully of God's people.

"Yeah, but Sister Thomas is so big she could be Goliath," Bobby said. "Anybody got a slingshot handy?"

My mother glared at him. "Apologize," she demanded.

"So sahree, Sister Thomas," Bobby said in a squeaky baby voice.

When I started laughing my mother pinched me, and it hurt. Suddenly the milk crate next to her didn't seem like the best seat in the house. Sister Thomas said that we would probably show more respect if we were required to wear our Sunday clothes for Bible study.

"When children dress up, they act different," she told my mother. "I mean we are coming before God during the study. It only makes sense to put on our best."

So, from that time on, we had to dress up for each study. Everybody blamed Bobby, for not only did we lose our Saturday, but we had to spend it wearing our most uncomfortable clothing.

My mother tried to give Sister Thomas "a few dollars" for the reading material, but she refused. "Just put it in the Worldwide Work box when you start coming to the Kingdom Hall," she said.

I thought Sister Thomas might get tossed out one Saturday, when she told my mother that a painting of baby cherubs on our living room wall was "of pagan origin."

"In every biblical account where angels appear, they always take the shape of a man," Sister Thomas said. "They are never shown as children or women, and certainly never lower creatures like dogs or cats," she added, glaring at me. The previous Saturday, in a deliberate attempt to rile her, I had asked if dogs and cats went to heaven. I didn't like Sister Thomas much—there was something phony about her. She always acted as if she was smarter than my mother but I knew full well that she was not.

After Sister Thomas informed my mother about the "pagan" cherubs, I expected my mother to give the sister her walking papers. Instead, my mother tilted her head, as if she was remembering the words of some long-forgotten song. After study that day, my mother took the cherub painting down off the wall, where it had hidden a ball-sized hole that

Bobby had made with his elbow one summer when he was learning how to do the funky chicken.

One Saturday, Sister Thomas brought over her husband, Brother Thomas. He laughed easily, and he was as short as his wife was tall. At almost five feet, I was about eye-to-eye with him. Brother Thomas's nose always seemed to be red. He said it was due to allergies, but I thought it was more likely caused by booze. Brother Thomas always smelled like beer.

One Saturday Brother Thomas gave my mother the gift of a plaque that read, As for me and my house, we will serve Jehovah. My mother hung the plaque over the hole in the wall.

On each visit Brother Thomas asked me to recite the books of the Bible in order. I had been doing so since I was five, but Brother Thomas still acted impressed every time. I liked him just a little bit better than I liked his wife.

And just when I thought we were going to have our Saturdays taken over for the rest of the year with Bible study, my mother stopped studying.

We had started going regularly to the Kingdom Hall on Sundays. My mother usually sat next to Sister Thomas and her husband. But one particular Sunday, Sister Thomas made a point of getting up halfway through the talk and moving over to the other side of the Kingdom Hall. Then Brother Thomas shifted over next to my mother, whispering something in her ear. During the break between the talk and the Watchtower lesson, my mother told me to get Mark and Mariah. We were leaving.

We rode the bus home in silence. I could guess that our abrupt departure had something to do with Brother Thomas but I couldn't guess what.

Then, that Monday, Sister Thomas came banging on our front door.

"Sister Gordon, I want to talk to you about Brother Thomas!" she yelled.

"Nobody want your crusty-ass man," my mother said,

throwing open the door. "You drunk? I know yo' man be drinking. You den got into the sauce too?"

"He ain't home every Friday night, and he say he over here," Sister Thomas cried.

"1 Corinthians 13:4 'Love is long-suffering and kind. Love is not jealous.'" My mother practically spat this scripture in Sister Thomas's face.

That stopped Sister Thomas in her tracks. She blinked as if something was just coming into view. Then she yelled, "You need to leave my man alone! He ain't home every Friday night. 'Let marriage be honorable among all,'" she said. "'And let the marriage bed be without defilement.' That's Hebrews 13:4."

"Look, heffa! Your man is over here because he's been studyin' with my son, Steven," my mother said, raising her voice to be heard over Sister Thomas's sobs. "And I'm working night shift on Friday! You might have asked befo' you started accusin' somebody, and makin' the congregation think I'm the kind of ho that would go after some married motherfuckah! Now get your stank-ass, trick-ass off my property," my mother yelled, slamming the door in her face.

Sister Thomas shuffled back to her car and drove away. We never saw her again. And we didn't go to the Kingdom Hall on Sundays after that.

My mother apparently blamed Brother Thomas for what happened, because he had let his wife believe that he was coming over for something other than Bible study.

"Crazy, ugly-ass fool probably just wanted her to believe somebody else was interested in his stupid fat ass," she said in a phone conversation with Ainey. "Fool was probably tryin' to make his big bitch jealous," she said. "Men so damned stupid whether they supposed to be Christian or not."

On Tuesday, when I came home from school, my mother was using the ashtray for its intended purpose. Our Saturdays were free again for a while. This Witness phase was complete.

Thirteen

The Brood Grows Up

Without Bible study to occupy us, we returned our focus to individual pursuits.

Steven graduated from "regular" high school, and so his father took him on a special trip over the weekend. We'd assumed they attended a wrestling match, but I later found out the truth of the matter. Bobby told me that Roy Randolph had taken Steven down to Tijuana to visit whores, but Steven was too shy to do anything with them. Meanwhile, Roy Randolph's other child, Yvonne, was starting to date a string of men. By the end of the eighties, she'd had six abortions. She told me that one of the procedures shouldn't count for two abortions because she had been pregnant with twins.

I asked her why she didn't get herself "fixed," instead of using abortion for birth control. She told me that she didn't want to be barren, should she ever meet Mr. Right.

"Who you kiddin'? Mr. Right don't want you," I told her.

She didn't speak to me for a month.

During this time, Cynthia became pregnant. She had a daughter and named her Little Sarah, after my mother.

A couple of years later my mother had Fred, my youngest brother. My mother was forty-seven years old at the time, and the new baby was added to the family without question.

"Well, at least Sarah has someone to grow up with," Cynthia said.

Cynthia often left Sarah in my mother's care when she was fighting with the baby's father, Derrick. During one such fight he tried to strangle her.

Meanwhile, Morris—who was two years younger than

me—talked for hours on the phone with his various male friends, discussing comic books and science fiction novels (or so I was told).

When Willie turned eighteen, he decided to join the army. The army would help him get a diploma. "You come for tutoring on Monday, Wednesday, and Friday, and you can get your GED. Then you can enlist," the recruiter told him. But Willie spent most of the weekdays watching soap operas, and he told the army recruiter that he couldn't give them up, even if it meant he couldn't get a high school diploma.

Bobby, too, went to a recruiting office and joined the army. He told me that he thought my mother's harsh training should have prepared him for the Armed Forces. I told him that there was a big difference between the army and our mother.

When he asked what that might be, I said, "Mama loves you and they don't."

Bobby got about halfway through his sixteen weeks of basic training before there was an incident.

He told us about it when he got home. "That sergeant had it in for me right from the start," Bobby said. "He was a big corn-fed, redneck motherfuckah. He wouldn't call me Bobby because he said that was a name for a baby who's still on the tit. There were two Bobs in the company, so I wound up being Black Bob. And everybody called me that."

Bobby described one early incident in basic training:

The sergeant was a big man with an even bigger voice. Bobby was almost six foot, and the sergeant looked down on him. It was as if he were a bear standing upright on his hind legs, Bobby said. And he had a habit of standing close so that you could feel his hot breath on your face.

During one browbeating, Bobby took a step back from the sergeant.

"Did I tell you to move, Black Bob?" the drill instructor shouted.

Bobby responded, "No, sir!"

"Then why did you move, Private?" the sergeant demanded. "That question wasn't rhetorical, you puke! You will respond and I do mean now! And it had better be the truth."

Bobby winced and waved his hand in front of his face, as
though fending off the sergeant's foul breath. "Poor Marge,"
he said, quoting from an old Listerine commercial, "she'll
never hold a man until she does something about her breath."

The entire company burst into laughter, and the drill sergeant couldn't get them back under control for several minutes. After that, the sergeant made it a point of tormenting
my brother every chance he got.

Finally, one morning the sergeant said to Bobby, "You
want to take a swing at me, don't you, Black Bob?"

Bobby smiled and kept his cool.

"Why are you smiling at me? You want to take me to the
prom or something? Well, I don't want to go to the prom
with some ugly Black bastard," the sergeant said.

Bobby stopped smiling.

Finally, one morning on parade the sergeant confronted
Bobby. "Is it all these witnesses at attention here that you're
worried about? I can fix that," the sergeant yelled. "Company
about face!"

On command, everybody but Bobby turned around.

"Now, they're no witnesses," he said. "What's wrong? You
scared of the big, bad sergeant? Look, I'll make it easy for
you. I'll put my hands behind my back."

Bobby knew that the sergeant wanted him to throw a
punch, so he could duck it and then beat him up. So instead
Bobby kneed him the groin, and when he bent over, Bobby
clipped him in the jaw, breaking it.

Bobby spent a week in the stockade before he was giv-
en something called a DD-214 or Certificate of Release or
Discharge from Active Duty that stated he had a "failure to
adapt."

Bobby stayed home for about a year, mostly eating and
watching TV.

About a year to the day after he was discharged from the army, Bobby went away to Job Corps, a job training program for the poor. While in the program he fell in love with a Japanese girl and proposed marriage. She told him that she'd never marry anyone who wasn't Japanese, nor would she marry a poor man.

When he returned home, Bobby spent hours listening to Michael Jackson's "She's Out of My Life," on his Walkman, singing loudly off-key.

He told my mother that it was all her fault that we were so poor. He tried leaving my mother's house several times, only to wind up spending the summer on Yvonne's couch. But when he stopped receiving General Relief welfare, Yvonne asked him to leave, and he was back at home with us.

My mother took him to several doctors until one recommended a psychiatrist, who started Bobby on Thorazine to treat his psychotic symptoms. He thought Bobby might have bipolar disorder and schizophrenia. Bobby took his meds for some time and then stopped. He told me they made him constipated and drowsy. He didn't tell my mother, who had been making sure he took them to curb his combative tendencies. She didn't find out he'd stopped taking them until he got into a major fight with Cynthia's boyfriend, Derrick, who was also dating two of her best friends. We'd been told, too, that he was already married to yet another woman. Cynthia was as combative with Derrick as she had been with me when we were growing up. But Derrick did much more to provoke her.

After Cynthia became pregnant with his child, Derrick began to give her money for child support. But he would turn around the next day and ask to "borrow" the money back, because he had a lead on a good poker game or a fast horse. Cynthia would give him back the money, and then they would fight when he didn't pay back the "loan."

After one altercation, Cynthia told Bobby that Derrick had attempted to strangle her, revealing finger marks on her throat. Bobby told her to invite Derrick over to our house, where Bobby punched him until he was rolling on the floor, and then he kicked in his teeth. There was blood everywhere. Bobby would probably have killed Derrick if my mother had not emerged from her room carrying her rifle.

"All right, motherfuckahs, that's enough," she said, cocking the gun. "You stupid bastards ain't gonna be breakin' up my shit."

My mother made Bobby take Derrick to the emergency room, where they made up some story about playing football and a fall in the yard. No police report was offered or taken. "Just a coupla niggers fightin'," said the cop to the ER nurse, who'd called the police. Bobby was relieved that they wouldn't be going to jail.

My mother told Bobby that either he went back on his meds or he had to move out. He went back on the meds.

Despite their battles and his other women, Cynthia moved in with Derrick. One night while I was visiting Yvonne, Cynthia phoned to say that Derrick's wife had returned, and she had fallen asleep on their sofa.

Yvonne flew into a rage when I told her about it.

"Mama didn't raise us to take this kind of bullshit off no man," she said. "Come on, we gotta go get our sister and our niece."

I knew if I didn't go along there would be even more mayhem. I went to keep us on mission. As I saw it, our mission was to get Cynthia and Little Sarah out safely. We had four bus changes as we traveled to Cynthia's house in Long Beach, and I took the time to reason with Yvonne.

"You gotta let me talk to him when we get there," I said.

"If he don't start nothin', ain't gonna be nothin'," she responded.

At five foot six, Yvonne was taller than me by four inches and weighed a solid 150 pounds. Even sitting down she looked like my big sister. She was chesty, like all my mother's girls, with a patrician nose. She once told me that our mother had pinched her nose every day when she was little, so her nose would be straight rather than flat and meaty like Steven's. Yvonne had dark super-smooth skin that she slathered with Noxzema cream every night. She wore her hair in long French braids to her shoulders. Some of the hair was real and some of it wasn't. No one could really tell the difference. Most people thought she was the best looking of my mother's daughters. Yvonne's good looks had always gotten her in and out of trouble. I wondered if her looks would be a factor in court when she was charged with the attempted murder of Derrick.

On the bus ride I noticed that she was breaking into a sweat. "How much have you had to drink tonight?" I asked.

"Shut up, girl," she responded. "I ain't had nothin' to drink."

"Did you have something else?" I asked.

"Ain't none of yo' damn business what I choose to do with my free time," she said, resting her head against the bus window. She was starting to doze, and I was sure that there was something in her system besides her go-to drink of Miller High Life beer. Yvonne could hold a lot of beer. I'd once purchased a case of twenty-four cans, and she'd polished them all off in one weekend, while cooking a delicious dinner for a dozen people. But when Yvonne took drugs, she became erratic, even dangerous. After one weekend crack-cocaine binge, she tried to set one of her boyfriends on fire by dousing him with lighter fluid and throwing matches at him. It was his good fortune that the matches went out before they reached him. His offense had been that he'd protested loudly and violently when she told him she had aborted his twins.

I sat quietly for the rest of the bus ride. I needed to form a plan about what to do if things started to go south at Cynthia's house.

When we arrived, Yvonne bounded off the bus. Cynthia's house was half a mile from the bus stop, and my sister ran the whole way. Breathless, she marched up to the front door, banged, and shouted, "Open up! It's the police!"

Derrick came to the door and opened it six inches, just the length of the chain. We could see his massive 300-pound bulk through the gap in the door. He wasn't wearing a shirt, and his belly hung over his partly zipped jeans. His eyes were bloodshot and weary.

"What the hell you doing here, Yvonne? And why you banging on my door like some lunatic?" Derrick said, with a pronounced Mike Tyson-like lisp.

I couldn't remember if he'd had the speech impediment before Bobby had kicked his teeth in.

"I want to see my sister," Yvonne said. "She said she needs help."

Derrick noticed that I was standing behind Yvonne. "Y'all ain't gonna do nothing stupid, right?" he addressed the question to me.

"We just want to talk to Cynthia," I said, stepping in front of Yvonne. "We just want to see if she needs help with the baby or something."

Derrick closed the door, and I could hear the scratching of the chain. The door opened a foot before Yvonne shoved me aside and rushed into the house.

"Where she at?" Yvonne yelled, and I knew she wasn't talking about our sister.

A rail-thin, barefoot, light-skinned woman in a red leather miniskirt and black tank top jumped up from the sofa. She wore a long blonde wig, which swayed when she rose, dwarfing her tiny frame. All I could think about was Cousin It from the *The Addams Family* TV show.

Yvonne headed toward her, but the woman was a blur of synthetic hair and elbows. She cleared the ottoman in one leap and headed for a door that I assumed was the bedroom. She slammed the door behind her, and I heard the lock click loudly on the other side. Yvonne banged on the door. "Get your skank ass out here," she yelled.

"Yvonne, you gotta get out of my house with all that yellin' and carryin' on."

I found Cynthia in a kitchen chair holding Sarah close to her chest. She was rocking and singing, "Hush little baby, don't say a word, Mama's gonna buy you a mocking bird."

"Girl, what's wrong with you?" I said. "Don't you hear all that commotion out there? We gotta go."

Cynthia looked up at me as if she were coming out of a deep sleep. She'd told members of the family that Derrick had spiked her food and water with Quaaludes to calm her down when she was becoming violent. I wondered if she had been dosed recently. I didn't want to stop to ask. I saw the diaper bag in the corner, and I started filling it with baby stuff.

"Where's your stuff?" I said, trying to shout over Yvonne's banging and Derrick's yelling in the other room.

"My stuff is in the bedroom," Cynthia said, her speech slurring. "I'll get it." She tried to rise with the baby in her arms, but then she sat down hard like it was all just too much.

"It's okay," I said. "We'll come back tomorrow. We gotta catch four buses so it's probably better that we don't have a lot of stuff anyway."

"My baby just got born," she said. "I cain't take her on no bus with all them dirty people. She gonna catch something."

I shook my head and went to the living room, still carrying the diaper bag. Yvonne banged on the bedroom door, calling down holy hell on the woman on the other side. Derrick had opened the front door and was telling Yvonne that she had better get out before he called the police.

Ignoring the bedlam, I told Derrick, "I need your keys so we can take Cynthia and the baby to Yvonne's house. I promise I'll get the car back to you tomorrow."

Just as Derrick was fishing out his keys, Yvonne got in his face. "You a stupid motherfuckah bringing this ho up in here with your woman and yo baby," she said.

"Ain't none of yo business how I run my house," Derrick

said. Pointing to the bedroom door, he continued, "That there is my friend, and she in trouble, and I ain't gonna turn her away just 'cause you say so."

Cynthia emerged from the kitchen, clutching Little Sarah to her chest. "Get him, Yvonne," she said.

Like a dog called to attack, Yvonne removed a knife from the back pocket of her jeans and ran full speed at Derrick with the knife outstretched in her fist. Derrick whipped me around, and held me as a shield in front of him. Yvonne was not deterred. She tried to reach around me and stab Derrick, but he was too fast. He hopped backward, out of the way of the blade, still holding me firmly by my shoulders, and pushing me out in front of him.

"Stop it!" I screamed at them both. But no one was listening to me. I was just an object to them. For Derrick I was little better than a lion tamer's chair; for Yvonne I was a smaller animal of minor concern, who was keeping her from her prey.

I thought that I was going to be killed. I tried to recall what I had planned before arriving at the house. It had something to do with getting the car keys and getting out before matters escalated. I couldn't seem to focus. My ears were ringing. My mouth was dry, and all I could think of was that I really wanted something to drink.

My body and Derrick's backward hops put him just out of reach of the knife. Yvonne was practically yelling in my ear. He alternated between calling Yvonne a "crazy bitch" and yelling for her to get the hell out of his house.

"I'ma kill you, motherfuckah!" Yvonne kept screaming.

Cynthia stood near the open front door, cuddling her baby and cooing to her softly. Was I going crazy or was she actually singing Little Sarah a lullaby while this was going on? I thought I heard Cynthia sing, "Hush little baby, don't say a word…" But I willed myself to focus on Yvonne as if my life depended on it.

My voice came out in a desperate croak. "Let's just go,

Yvonne," I said. But she had gone completely red zone, and I don't think she heard me. The drugs and the adrenaline had taken over. Yvonne stared past me, trying to find an opening that would allow her to stab at Derrick. I moved my head back and forth in an attempt to get her to look me in the eyes.

"Let's just go," I said, between clenched teeth. "Let's go."

Derrick held my shoulders from behind. He was stronger than he looked and I couldn't wriggle from his grasp. I grabbed Yvonne's shoulders as she stood in front of me. I was sandwiched between them. Derrick backed up just out of reach of the blade's thrust as Yvonne moved forward.

Yvonne could not seem to focus on me, but I focused on her. Then Derrick suddenly stopped moving. I felt Derrick's grip loosen on my shoulders. He glanced behind him at the white plaster wall.

I saw my chance and let go of Yvonne's shoulders. I dropped into a crouch. At that moment, Yvonne switched her grip on the knife, raising it overhead to stab Derrick in the chest. I threw up the diaper bag to protect myself, and I felt the force of the blade on top of my head like a fist. The knife caught on something in the bag, and Yvonne spent the next few seconds trying to yank it out. Standing up, I shoved Yvonne in the chest as hard as I could. She fell over the ottoman, and I tossed the bag with the knife wedged in it toward the open door and out of her reach.

"All right! All right! Goddamnit!" I shouted, like a bouncer in a seedy bar. "That's enough of this bullshit!" Derrick and Yvonne glared at each other like boxers between rounds. "Gimme those goddamn keys before this crazy-ass bitch kills you," I said to Derrick.

Yvonne had gotten off the floor and was heading for the knife that was sticking out of the bag.

"You want to go to jail for killing this good-for-nothing loser?" I screamed at her.

I noticed the keys had fallen on the floor during the

struggle and I scooped them up. Cynthia was already out the front door, the baby in one arm and the knife-pierced diaper bag over her shoulder. The bag dripped white liquid from a can of Similac baby formula.

"I'll get the keys back to you tomorrow," I told Derrick hoarsely. I grabbed Yvonne's hand and led her backward from the room.

I drove cab-driver style because Yvonne, still smarting from the shove I'd given her, refused to ride in the passenger seat. She joined Cynthia and Little Sarah on the back bench of Derrick's old station wagon.

In the rearview mirror I could see that Yvonne was sleeping and Cynthia, with Little Sarah on her chest, was also starting to look sleepy. And it struck me that the baby had not cried once during the entire ordeal, as if such fights were an everyday occurrence.

"What's the appeal?" I asked Cynthia. "Derrick's ugly, fat, stupid, and broke, and he's got other women, right? And he's got a gambling problem, right? What do you see in this loser?"

"I want more babies," she said, as if that explained everything.

"Uh, that doesn't answer my question," I said.

"I don't want to do what Mama did and have babies from different fathers," she said. "It's too confusing for them."

"And this ain't?" I said. "You mean to tell me that you don't want to make Mama's mistakes, so you're making bigger mistakes? Tell me how that makes sense."

Cynthia sucked her teeth, and shut her eyes. She was asleep in minutes.

Later that night, Derrick came to pick up Cynthia, his daughter, and his car.

After that, I refused to get involved in any more of Cynthia's domestic squabbles.

I started to apply to colleges. I had graduated as the valedictorian of Compton High School, and one of my teachers told me that there was a full scholarship waiting for me at Fisk University in Tennessee, if I wanted to go to a historically Black college. I told my mother about it.

"I struggled to get my babies out of the South, and now one of them wants to go back on her own," she said.

"A full scholarship is a lot of money," I told her, "and I'll be home for all the holidays."

"Why you want to move way, way from your old mama?"

I decided that it was probably best to stay on the West Coast, and I was accepted at the University of Southern California with a partial scholarship. I would have to take out loans to pay for the rest, but I had to stay close to my mother. I wanted to be there for her, if she needed me. The university was ten miles and one bus ride away, but a world away from South Central L.A. I could come home every weekend or any time during the week for emergencies.

My mother was sick on and off during my first semester. I asked her how the doctor was treating her, and she told me that the old family doctor, Dr. Bennett, had stopped accepting Medi-Cal welfare payments, so she'd had a new doctor every few months.

"They can't do that," I protested.

"Yeah, they can, Mary," my mother said. "Poor people ain't got no rights. Read this here."

She shoved a pamphlet in my hand. The title on the gray cover read, Your Evidence of Coverage and Membership Handbook. In the lower left-hand corner, a stick figure family held hands over a United Health Plan logo.

"They said that if a doctor no longer accepts UHP or Medi-Cal, I gotta find one that do, and that's hard," she said. "I gotta do five bus changes to get to a doctor."

"Mama, I can borrow a car from one of my friends, and I can take you to your doctor's appointment."

"You got your own life," she said.

"Yeah, but you're still part of it. Will you do something for me? If you're not going to let me drive you around to appointments, can you at least write down all your health problems? You can take that to any new doctors so they have a consistent record of your health problems. This is important, Ma."

Later that week, my mother gave me a list of her many ailments and asked me to proofread it.

In my mother's beautiful spider script, the list read:

Complaints of Sarah Gordon:

Leg pain while walking four or more blocks.

Back and leg pain in morning when I get up.

Bleeding gums.

Left eye some sight loss.

Chronic hypertension that requires the constant use of diuretics, beta blockers, potassium.

Inability to lift more than thirty pounds. Puts strain on old hernia scar.

Broken veins in both legs, sometimes painful.

Painful fibroids in abdomen.

Frequent headaches.

Tingling in fingertips and toes intermittently.

My mother continued her woes on a separate sheet of paper that had been torn from a spiral steno-pad notebook.

Operations:

August 1970. I had a light put on my bladder to regulate urinary flow. I had it done on 120th and Broadway. It was at Bon Aire hospital. The doctor's name was Frome.

October 1982. I had a ruptured (hernia) abdominal area. I was five months pregnant. The doctor had to go in and repair the hernia with the fetus inside. U.S.C. medical center Women's Clinic.

After the birth of my last son in 1983, I began having dizzy spells every time I bent over.

I finished reading the list, the pages crumpled in my hand as I choked back tears.

"Mama, please, please let me take you to the doctor," I begged.

"I applied for the paratransit, and I'm gonna get it," my mother said. "They can take me to the doctor. They got that nice air-conditioned bus that picks you up right at your door.

"What about other errands?" I asked.

"If you really want to do something, you can come and get me on the first and the fifteenth and take me grocery shopping."

When my friends grew tired of my borrowing their cars, I purchased a fifteen-year-old Plymouth Volare for $400. It was blue with more primer than paint and got about ten miles to the gallon. I called it the Blue Bomber. With it I was able to take my mother on her shopping trips.

The shopping trips reminded me of the old days with Nellybelle. But it wasn't quite like the old days because I was older, and so was my mother. The years were wearing on her and on me.

When my mother was feeling especially unsteady, I took the list from her and went shopping in the ABC market.

One such list read: (1) chicken parts (2) turkey parts (3) pork chops (4) canned milk (5) sugar (6) potatoes (7) oxtails (8) canned peaches (9) bacon (10) coffee (11) tea (12) large soda pop (13) washing powder (14) shortening (15) eggs (16) milk and (17) cheese.

There were no fresh fruit or vegetables on the list. I asked my mother about this. She made no apologies for how she chose to eat.

"Girl, you know that down here in the ghetto they ain't got no fresh nothing to eat," she said. "They want to sell you rotten or near-rotten fruit and vegetables if you shop down here, and there ain't no other place to shop no way. I ain't gonna pay full price for rotten shit."

"Okay, that's fair but Ma, are you sure you should be eating these pork chops with your high blood pressure?" I asked.

"I didn't ask for your two cents on my list. You ain't running nothing but yo' mouth," she said. "I can sit here for a minute and get my legs back under me, and I can go do my own damn shopping." I scurried into the market before my mother could take the list from me and filled the order.

During our shopping trips, my mother filled me in on family matters. Only Yvonne and I lived away from home.

My mother was responsible for Cynthia's newborn, Little Sarah; four-year-old Fred; nine-year-old twins, Mark, and Mariah; thirteen-year-old Teresa; sixteen-year-old Willie; eighteen-year-old Morris; twenty-two-year-old Cynthia; twenty-four-year-old Bobby; and twenty-eight-year-old Steven.

"I've been taking Cynthia to the Kingdom Hall lately," she said.

"Did she ask to go?"

"Naw, none of you have taken to the Truth like I wanted," my mother said. "But I got to take her because she said she been hearing voices."

"Voices?"

"She said the voices are telling her to kill her baby," she said. "Now only a demon would tell a mama to kill they baby. So I been taking her to hear God's word. That's a voice that she needs to hear."

I sighed. "Ma, what about taking her to see a professional, like a psychiatrist or something?"

"All they want to do is blame the mama and give her more drugs," she said. "I'm already doing all what I can to help that chile. And until she gets right, I'm gonna make sure nothing happens to my grandbaby."

I sighed again. "You're already taking care of Cynthia, her baby, and all of the rest of them," I said.

"Those my children," she said. "Ain't I suppose to take care of them? The same way I would take care of you, if you was in trouble."

"Don't worry about me. If I get pregnant before I graduate, I'll just give the baby up for adoption," I said.

"You do that, Mary, and I'll never forgive you," she said. "Ain't no cause for no orphanages or whatever the hell they call them these days, when you got people who are willing to care for you."

I started to remind her that she had considered adoption for the twins once. Then, I decided to change the subject. "How's Morris?" I asked.

"That boy so damn cheap," she said. "He don't want to pay no phone bill, but he spend all day and night on the phone with his friends talking about those comic books like he some damn kid. And sometimes he goes through my stuff in my room when I ain't there. He lookin' for money or something. That boy is a damned sneak thief."

"And Willie?" I asked.

"He got that General Relief welfare money, and he bought one of those VCR things, and all he do is watch movies and eat. You cain't get him off the couch. He's getting as big as a house. And you know he still hooked on them damned soap operas. Calls 'em his stories."

Moving on, I thought. "You heard from Big Willie?" I asked.

"Oh, you ain't heard," she said. "He real, real sick in the hospital. It's lung cancer. You should go see him before he passes."

"Why didn't anybody tell me?" I said.

"You all busy with school and everything, and you know his wife real snotty about being the stepmama to Teresa and Little Willie, and the rest of y'all ain't nothing to her," she said.

I decided that I'd heard enough family gossip, so I rode the rest of the way in silence and helped my mother get the bags out of the car. In the house, everyone was watching a rerun of *Full House*.

"I'm gonna make some oxtail stew," my mother said, not seeming to notice that no one was helping her put the food away. "That's your favorite, ain't it, Mary? Stay for dinner."

I told my mother I couldn't stop for dinner because I wanted to go visit Big Willie in the hospital. But I didn't go to see Big Willie. It was all just too sad. He had only been my stepfather for five years of my life, but he was the only father I'd ever known, and certainly the only one I'd ever loved.

I drove the Blue Bomber home to my clean, safe university apartment, where I only had to contend with a roommate. I had every intention of seeing Big Willie in the hospital the following weekend, but midweek, my mother told me that he'd died.

His widow did not invite us to the funeral. She didn't like us, Bobby said, because Big Willie had often referred to my mother as "the love of his life."

Although my college was less than ten miles from my mother's house, it might as well have been a world away. I read an obituary about my mother's friend Bill in the local weekly paper about three weeks after the memorial had taken place. It had been a year since I had last seen him. He'd offered to work on the Blue Bomber.

"Dat thing coughing like a dying dog, Mary," he told me. "Let old Bill tune it up for you."

Bill had survived on odd jobs and welfare for decades. I told him that I couldn't give him his standard fee of a carton of cigarettes and a case of beer, but I'd get him a pint of J&B whiskey. "School is kicking my ass with all these fees," I said.

"You is fambly," he said. "You pay me when you can."

I asked Bill what he had been up to. "I been going to see a doctor," he said. "He said I got something wrong with my internals. He told me that I gotta stop drinking."

Immediately I felt guilty about the offer of whiskey. "Bill, maybe you should do what the doctor says," I told him. "They go to school a long time to learn that stuff."

"Don't gimme none of yo' monkey motion, girl," he said. "You pups go to school and you think everybody who don't go to school is a fool. Why should I do what dat pipsqueak white boy tell me to do? I been having a nip ever since I was a diaper baby. My grandpappy lived ta be 100 and he had a big jar of corn mash every day of his life."

The following month the obituary in the local newspaper said Bill had died of liver failure.

When I was little, every adult seemed to care so much about what I said, and now, as an adult, no one seemed to listen to me at all. It was now my job to listen, I told myself.

I encouraged my mother to tell me about the family during our shopping trips, even if the stories were hard to hear.

She told me that Teresa, my fourteen-year-old sister, had been arrested for armed robbery and attempted murder. On July 4th, one of those hot, fry-an-egg-on-a-sidewalk days in Los Angeles, Teresa and her friend Monique wanted to have an Independence Day picnic at the beach, just like thousands of other people in the city. Monique was a mass of rolling flesh. She wore coveralls and wife-beater undershirts with no bra underneath. She told everyone who would listen that she "went commando"—or without underwear—because her girlfriend preferred to be able to take Monique's clothes off quickly for sex. One strap of her overalls hung down her back, along with a long black braid. Her expensive tennis shoes had been acquired at knifepoint from some other kid in the neighborhood. The shoelaces were always untied, and the tongues of the shoes lolled out.

The caper that got the girls in hot water apparently began as follows:

"Where we gonna get some scratch for our picnic?" said Monique.

"I think we should go down to that chink and jack him," Teresa said.

"You talking about Kim over at the Jones Market at the corner?" Monique said. "He ain't no chink. He's a gook and that crazy bastard keep a shotgun under the counter."

Jones Market had actually been owned by the Jones family at one time. According to people in the neighborhood, the Joneses were the last white people to live in the area. The seventies had been an era of white flight to suburbs like the San Fernando Valley. The store had changed hands at least a dozen times, and most of those hands had been Korean since the early eighties.

The current owner was Mr. Kim, who allowed some of the neighborhood to pay on credit. Knowing this, Teresa thought it worth a try and less risky than robbery. So she said, "Hey, Mr. Kim, let us get some bread and soda and stuff for a picnic, and we gonna pay you next week."

"No give credit to kids," Mr. Kim told her.

"Then what about those county bitches with welfare checks," Monique countered. "Plenty of them hos is under eighteen."

"Yeah, but I know they got income," he said. "They come in here and cash they checks."

"Yeah, and you charge them five dollars and sometimes ten dollars for it, don't you?" Teresa said.

"Me got to make profit some way," he said. "Me no bank."

"Let's get the fuck out of here," Teresa said. "This gook fool ain't gonna give us nothin'."

A Mexican woman with a small child exited after them. The woman walked six blocks to a bus stop. The weight of her baggage pulled down her left shoulder, and the grip on her toddler's hand pulled down her right.

"Let's jack that bitch," Monique said.

Teresa and Monique stepped in front of the woman, who dropped her shopping bags and held her child close to her.

"Give us yo money," Monique said.

"No hablo ingles," the woman replied.

Monique grabbed the toddler in a headlock and put a knife to its temple and said, "You hablo ingles, now?"

"I only got food stamps," the woman said in English.

"Then give us yo motherfuckin' food stamps," Teresa said. "And give us that shit in yo' shopping bags too."

The woman handed over her purse and her groceries. They let the child go.

They took the food stamps to the nearest ABC supermarket, purchased enough food for a picnic, and then caught the bus to the beach. They came back with nothing but the stolen purse, which they hid under a pile of clothing in my mother's closet.

Later that day three police cars arrived at Jones Market. Mr. Kim was able to stand on the corner and point to my mother's house where he knew Teresa lived.

Not knowing what had transpired that day at Jones Market, my mother met the officers at the door and said, "Come on in and search the place. We ain't got nothing to hide."

After the officers found the purse, they led everyone in the house at gunpoint into the front yard. Everyone, including my four-year-old brother, was told to lie face down in the grass with their hands clasped behind their heads.

In the back seat of one of the police cars was the Mexican woman Teresa and Monique had robbed, and her teenage son. Seeing Teresa and Monique in the yard, he leaped out of the car and tried to attack them. "You fucking putas," he shouted. "You robbed my mom."

The police tackled him before he could reach Teresa and Monique. They tried to make a run for it, and they, too, were tackled, handcuffed, and carted away. They stayed in jail until the trial because no one could post their $10,000 bail.

Yvonne attended the trial.

"They was yelling and screaming stuff at the judge," Yvonne told me afterward.

"What stuff?" I asked.

"Teresa and that other idiot kept saying stuff like, 'We know where you park your car,'" Yvonne said. "Then the judge asked if any adults in the court would take responsibility for Teresa, but Mama didn't say nothin'. And I damn sure wasn't going to speak up if Mama didn't."

Fourteen-year-old Teresa was sent to juvenile detention until she turned eighteen. Her accomplice received a similar sentence.

I asked my mother why she didn't speak up in court.

"I figured that the way this girl was going, she was going

to get herself killed on those streets," she said. "I figured that if she went to jail, she would have a few more years to grow up and maybe get herself straightened out."

"Ma, some people are just sociopaths," I said. "There's nothing you can do to help them."

"Is that the kind of bullshit they teaching you in college?" my mother said. "They teaching you to give up on your people? And she ain't just some people; she is my baby and your sister. That girl is going to get her shit together when she's in lockup. That happens sometimes."

And sometimes, I thought, people come out of jail worse criminals than when they went in.

Months later I was visiting my mother one weekend. I stepped into the dimly lit kitchen to find my mother sitting at the battered wooden table, puffing on a homemade cigarette, her left hand resting on a .38-caliber Smith and Wesson.

"Is that thing loaded?" I asked.

"Of course it's loaded," my mother said. "Ain't no use of having a gun that ain't loaded."

I thought that the teenage son of Teresa's robbery victim had been coming around, so she had her gun ready. "Ma, if that Cholo guy comes around here, you should report it to the police," I said.

My mother gazed toward the window. And for the first time I noticed that there was plywood where the window should have been.

"Do you know this is the same kind of gun that Marvin Gaye's father used to kill his son?" my mother said.

"No, I didn't know that," I said. "Ma, what's happened?"

"Bobby been coming around here and busting out my windows and calling me all kinds of bitches. He done gone off his medication again, and I cain't put up with it."

I sat down opposite my mother. Her eyes were bloodshot, and the wrinkles in her forehead seemed deeper. The nails on her hands were bitten down so far past the quick that they had started to bleed. There were bloody fingerprints on the dozen or so butts in the ashtray in front of her. And my mother, who had always been proud of having her hair just so, had allowed some long grey strands to pop out from her updo. They hung like a fly strip over her lazy left eye.

I remembered what one of my third-grade schoolmates said to me one night at a parent-teacher function: "Hey, your mother is cross-eyed."

And at eight years old, it was as if I was seeing my mother's defective eye for the first time. I asked my mother about getting it fixed, and she said the doctor told her that he could probably repair it, but there was a 50 percent chance of losing sight in the eye if he operated.

"I ain't entering no pageants or nothing, so I don't need my left eye to look pretty," she said. "I just need it to work. What if they fix it so that it looks pretty, but I cain't see out of the damn thing?"

My mother was always practical about such things. And now I tried to get her to see reason about the situation with Bobby.

"Ma, have you put in a police report about the window?"

"I called them. They said it's a civil matter, and I got to evict him," she said.

"So, you gonna take the law into your own hands and shoot Bobby like Marvin Senior did his son?"

"I don't want to shoot one of my own babies," she said. "But that boy is out of control like I said. You ain't seen the bedroom yet. I had Fred sleeping in my bed, and Bobby threw this big rock, must have been twenty-five pounds, through the bedroom window, and the rock landed just a few inches from Fred's head. That baby got cut with glass. He coulda kilt that little boy or anybody else."

"You could get a restraining order," I suggested. "And then the police have to take him if he comes over here."

She shook her head and replied, "Bobby ain't gonna let himself be taken by no police. You know what happened to him when he went to Arizona."

Actually, I didn't know. I had been preparing to go on a semester abroad in England, and I hadn't visited the family in months.

"What happened, Ma?" I asked.

"Bobby say that they locked him up for vagrancy in one of those little desert towns, and when he was sleeping, two of those cops came in and raped him."

"You believe that?"

"Yeah, I believe it," she said. "Ain't no man gonna lie about being raped if he wasn't. He said if the cops ever try to take him again, he gonna make them shoot him. They even got a name for it—suicide by cop."

"You think Bobby is trying to commit suicide by coming over here?"

"Yeah," my mother said. "Somebody in Marvin's family was with him when he died. And that guy told the papers that Marvin made his father shoot him because he couldn't do it himself." She paused. "Maybe his daddy just saw it as putting him out of his misery."

"Mama, there's got to be another way," I said.

My mother sighed heavily, scraped the chair back, and went to a kitchen drawer. She came back with one of her many steno pads that she used to write poetry and grocery lists. She started to write a letter to the court.

She wrote: "The police department claim the law allows people freedom to come into your house where you pay rent, to break a window with a boulder, but not with a brick, to cut a small child with glass, to stomp your front door nearly open, cussing and screaming dirty lies all over the neighborhood about you. Mr. Cotton says he doesn't fear anyone, not the LAPD, his family, or death. But we do fear these things."

My hand shook as I read the letter. It was the beginning of her request for a restraining order. She was telling the court as best she could that Bobby was completely out of control. And unlike Teresa, she couldn't wait for Bobby to simply be locked up. With Teresa, my mother's actions had been passive. She just didn't speak up in court on Teresa's behalf. With Bobby, she had to act against one of her children. For my mother to admit that something was hopeless for one of her brood was a great defeat, and I knew this. I wanted to relieve her of some of the burden.

"I can take it down there in the morning," I said.

"No, I can do it," she said. "I'll go down there tomorrow."

Later that week, my mother was given a temporary restraining order against her second son. One night he tried to enter our mother's house through the back door, and he was arrested. The judge ordered him to be taken to a mental institution for thirty days.

"All I can do now is pray that he stay away and find some kind of help," she said. "It helps to know that you ain't the only one with troubles. It reminds you to pray for everybody," she said, showing me a list she had been keeping for the past month.

Under the heading Food for Thought, she had listed a string of neighborhood tragedies she'd been keeping track of.

Six-year-old girl and her father killed over a baseball cap, killer riddled the house with bullets.

Eleven-year-old boy shot in head after mother puts gang member out of her house.

Two girls gunned down because of mistaken identity.

Man kills wife on Ninety-Fourth and Main Street at phone booth. Five kids motherless.

Girl, aged nine, burns up in house fire.

Torture, rape of the woman at a drug rock house.

Mistaken shooting of family at Fifty-Fourth Street.

Fifty-Fourth Street party, five killed and seven wounded.

After I finished reading the woeful account of neighborhood catastrophes, I tried a more direct approach. "Ma, you ever think about just getting out of here?" I said. "I mean you could take the little kids and just go. I mean besides Mark and Mariah, everybody else is a legal adult."

"I ain't just responsible for the little kids," she said. "I'm the mama and the daddy and I got to take care of everybody that I can."

Well, at least there was going to be one less responsibility, I thought. I had been putting off telling my mother that I was going to spend a semester abroad.

"Ma, I have to tell you something," I began. "I'm going to be away for a few months. There's an opportunity to spend a semester abroad in England. and I think I'm going to take it."

"You ain't gonna be safe over there," she said. "You read the papers just like I do. They got all kinds of trouble with terrorists over there. They bombed some big store called Harrods in London, and some people died."

"I know, Ma, but there's trouble all over the world," I said. "Just look at your list. There's no end of killing and violence in South Central. You can't tell me I'm gonna be safe here, even if I hide under the bed twenty-four-seven."

My mother shook her head and lit another cigarette. She puffed out the words, "You gonna call your old mama once a week when you gone."

"Sure, Ma, I'll do that."

I hugged my mother. And for the first time in my life, she hugged me back. That was as close as I was going to come to a blessing.

Once in London, I forgot to call once a week as I'd promised. My head was full of tube rides, museums, theatre, and field trips to the English countryside. During spring break I went to Paris and Madrid and practiced my French and Spanish. No one was more surprised than I was that I could actually use the right words to get around. I traveled alone because the other USC students in London were wealthy, and they had been to Paris and Madrid dozens of times, or so they said. They told me that those places had been "done to death." They preferred Amsterdam, where they could buy hashish over the bar. I didn't do drugs so such trips held little appeal for me.

While in London, I received several polite letters from my mother. According to her, everyone was doing fine. She always signed them Your mother, Sarah Gordon.

Just as I was about to return to the States, there was a shooting in a building near my classroom in London. Yvonne Joyce Fletcher, a British police officer, was fatally shot during a protest outside the Libyan embassy.

I was attempting to go to class, and a British bobby—in one of those ridiculous hats that always reminded me of old Keystone Cops movies—prevented me from going to my European Economy class in St. James Square.

"Where are you going, love?" he asked.

"My class is in that building over there," I told him, pointing.

"Oh, love, you can't go down there," he said. "There's been a spot of trouble."

"What happened?"

"Some nasties shot an officer near the embassy," he said.

"That's too bad," I said. "But that's the building next door."

I tried to walk around him, and he threw up a warning hand. "The whole area is cordoned off," he said. "They probably won't let you in St. James for a while. Now run along, there's a good lass," he said, shooing me off gently.

A shooting of one police officer and the whole country goes berserk, I thought. Could they even imagine what went on in South Central? I guess it was to be expected, since English cops didn't carry guns. I caught a double-decker bus to the nearest movie theater, and I went to see the movie *Footloose* and the live performance of *Evita*.

There was a telephone message for me back at the flat.

"Your mother called," my roommate told me. "I think you're in trouble."

The message scrawled on a piece of lined notebook paper read, *Call home!*

My mother had spent money to call another continent. It

must be important. The only available phone was a public one in the hallway, but a long line of people were waiting to use it. So I jogged to the red phone booth at the corner. It cost ten American dollars to talk for just a few minutes.

"Hello, Ma, it's me," I said. "What's going on?"

"You know what the hell happened," my mother said. "They shot some cop over there, and it's right next to that building where you go to school. I saw it on the news!"

"Oh, Ma, I'm so sorry. I should have called right away," I said. "I'm fine. Everyone is fine."

"When you coming home?"

"In just a few more weeks, Ma. I'm sorry I haven't been writing or calling," I said. "I'll do better."

And I did do better. I called home once a week. She always gave me the same reassuring message that everyone was just fine and everything was okay.

I wish, in retrospect, that I had told my mother to just spit it out. I wish I had told her that she could talk to me about stuff, even if I couldn't do a damn thing about it. We could talk the way we had on those shopping trips, even if I was thousands of miles away.

No one came to LAX to meet my plane. Everyone else had somebody waiting for them. One of my friends' parents even brought the family dog. I caught a cab to my mother's house. And I gave the driver three twenty-dollar bills, the last of my American money. The first thing I noticed was that the window had been repaired. The second thing I noticed was that the grass in the front lawn was four feet high. Clearly, Cynthia hadn't been mowing. The front porch—the graveyard for all discarded furniture—held a brown sofa with the velvet sheen worn off. A yellow diaper pail, overflowing with Pampers, sat on the other end of the porch, buzzing with flies. They made a sound like a live wire. There was a persistent smell of a backed-up toilet.

The cab driver came up behind me and set my suitcase next to the sofa.

"Oh, thanks, I almost forgot." He offered me my five dollars in change.

"No, you keep it," I said.

He was a squat Indian man in a turban. I had asked five drivers to take me to the address in South Central Los Angeles, and they had all said they were occupied or waiting for someone else. The driver curled the money to his chest as if it were a precious jewel, then ran to his cab that was idling at the curb.

In the living room, clothes and dirty dishes were scattered everywhere. Five of my siblings were watching a rerun of *Hogan's Heroes*. They barely looked up as I entered.

At that moment in my life, I felt left out of something. When we were kids, my mother used to sit for hours with hot and cold combs to style my sisters' hair. She would sit hunched in a kitchen chair as my sisters sat lotus-style with their backs to her. My hair had always been short, like a boy's, so I didn't get braids, ponytails, or perms. I didn't want the hairstyling, but I didn't want to be left out, either. I had wanted the closeness of sitting between my mother's knees while she slathered grease on my scalp and transformed my hair into something other than my kinky little Afro. But I was different then, and I was different now. And it had nothing to do with my time in London.

My mother came out of her bedroom. I hugged her, but she didn't hug me back. Her hair was grayer than I remembered. "Girl, why didn't you call? I would have met you at the airport," she said.

She went into the living room and shouted at my siblings: "Y'all turn that bullshit off and come say hi to your sister."

Without turning around, my siblings grunted something that could have been "welcome back." They were looking at the television as if it contained a hypnotic pinwheel.

"I'm sorry, there's been a lot going on," my mother said.

I shrugged. "Can I get some coffee? This jet lag is kicking my ass."

My mother sucked her teeth and headed toward the kitchen. I could almost hear her thoughts. *This little heffa done walked right up into my house and started cursing.*

I apologized for my crude language as my mother unwrapped the cord from the percolator. I had brought my mother a Mr. Coffee drip coffeemaker the previous year. She thanked me but never removed it from the box. She said the percolator made stronger coffee. *No need to try new stuff when the old stuff works just fine or better,* she'd said.

"You want to show me all your pictures and stuff from over there?" she asked.

"It's way down in the suitcase. Maybe tomorrow," I said. "I'm fried."

"What you up to now?" she asked.

I told her about my summer work-study job at Registration and Records at USC, and that I had campus housing set up. But I didn't really feel like talking about my next move. What mattered to me was what was going on at home. I wanted to jump up and shout: Enough small talk! What the hell is going on here?

Instead, I said, "Where's Cynthia?"

"Cynthia is at Augustus Hawkins," she said.

The Hawkins Mental Health Facility had opened in the neighborhood just a few years before.

"I been praying and praying about that chile, but she just so damn sad all the time," she said. "It's like ever since she had her baby, she just sad about every damn thing. She just cry and cry over nothing. They say this sometimes happen to young mothers."

To old ones too, I almost said. There were two preschoolers in the house: Cynthia's daughter, Sarah, and my brother Fred. My mother had been forty-seven when Fred was born. No one had ever met Fred's father. All we knew was that he was probably Puerto Rican or Mexican and my mother had had a brief affair with the man after meeting him in a downtown movie theater.

"And Cynthia wouldn't let me out of her sight," she said. "That girl is in her twenties, and she stand outside the bathroom till I'm done doing my business. She just ain't herself, and she was talking crazy about killing herself."

"Do you go to see her?"

"Yeah, I try to make it up there every day," she said. "I'm going up there tomorrow because the doctors want to talk to me."

I told my mother that I was going to visit a friend, and I would be back the next day. We would go to Augustus Hawkins together, I suggested.

My friends let me crash on their couch. I didn't wake up until five p.m. the following day, when I called my mother.

"Where you at?" she demanded. "Visiting hours is almost up."

"I'm sorry, Ma," I said. "I overslept. A friend of mine is going to drive me over and drop us both off at Augustus Hawkins."

We entered the large tan government building of many locked glass doors. It seemed library quiet to me. I don't know what I expected. I thought that it would be like a movie mental institution, where everyone was raving and trying to escape. But the only sound was the patients' slippers sliding across the tile floor, like sticks across the surface of a snare drum. The smell of pine cleaner and rubbing alcohol threatened to curl the hair in my nostrils. There were patients in every chair and a few on the common-room sofa watching a rerun of *The Addams Family*. I had to stop myself from singing, "They're creepy, and they're kooky..." Most of the patients were wearing hospital gowns, open at the back, and paper slippers. No one looked particularly distressed, although some had an expression of annoyance, as if they had received a call that interrupted their dinner.

Cynthia was sitting with her head down in the corner of the room. She was wearing a white bathrobe with giant fall leaves on it and matching slippers. My mother said she'd bought the sleepwear. If the patients had their own pajamas, the hospital staff knew that someone cared for them, she said.

I called to Cynthia, and she looked up. She had the face of a child. I marveled at how she'd been able to use her discount bus pass years after she had graduated high school. Always small, Cynthia now seemed to be engulfed in the robe, her form barely visible under the terrycloth.

"How they treating you, baby?" my mother said.

"Okay, Ma. I like the Jell-O," Cynthia said, her voice slurring, her eyes glassy.

"What kind of drugs they got you on?" I asked.

"Don't know," she said. "I take what they give me."

An announcement came on over the public address system. "Please make your way to the exit. Visiting hours are now concluded."

"I ain't even talked to the doctor yet," my mother said. "Don't worry, Cynthia. I'm gonna come back tomorrow. Give your sister a hug."

The command was directed at us both. And for a moment, I was transported back to all those childhood fights and the obligatory hugs after we had been punished. Now I hugged my sister tightly to my chest. I felt guilty for all those times that I had done it under silent protest. I whispered in her ear, "Don't let the bastards grind you down." I wanted to say it in the Latin that I had learned recently, but I knew she wouldn't understand it. Cynthia returned my embrace. We stood there hugging like long-lost friends, until a security officer came over and said visiting hours were over.

On the bus ride home, my mother told me that I didn't have to go to Augustus Hawkins with her the following day. I didn't go, but I swore to whatever higher power was listening that I was going to be a better sister. I thought I could help her get a life. I could help her get organized and maybe even find a purpose. First we would get her some real psychiatric help, not just drugs, I thought.

I didn't get the chance to help Cynthia. She came home changed. She was infuriatingly passive most of the time. Unlike Bobby, she took her pills religiously. The medication made her sleepy and incapable of following a logical train of thought. If you asked her how her daughter was doing in preschool, she would tell you what Little Sarah had had for dinner.

I had plenty of siblings. I could be a better sister to someone else, I thought. I'll start with Yvonne and work my way down.

I helped my oldest sister enroll in Southwest Community College. She told me that she wanted to be a secretary, so I enrolled her in typing, remedial math, and remedial reading. I helped her to navigate the arcane world of financial aid. But as soon as she got her grant money, she started skipping school. Then she was caught cheating in one of her classes and thrown out of the community college system altogether. After that she went into a drug spiral that included crack cocaine and cases of Miller High Life beer.

I called in a few favors from friends and got her a spot in a drug and alcohol rehabilitation center. But they sent over a male social worker to do the intake, and then they told me that there had been "inappropriate contact" with the social worker, and Yvonne's spot had been given away.

"You know what they say, Mary," my mother said. "You cain't help nobody until they admit they have a problem."

FOURTEEN

Survivor's Guilt

I graduated from the University of Southern California with a degree in journalism and a minor in international relations. My mother attended the graduation, and she brought along my five-year-old brother Fred. My mother said some of my other siblings had wanted to attend but they were "busy."

I began my career as a journalist at a little newspaper in Simi Valley, California, and was later offered a job at a larger newspaper in Las Vegas. I took it. My visits to my family were reduced to once a year at Christmastime.

One Christmas Teresa was fresh out of jail, and my mother asked me to take Teresa to Las Vegas to live with me. "Yvonne got Teresa slinging drugs out of her house. So she can pay for her own damn habit," my mother told me. "They both gonna get kilt messin' with that stuff."

I offered my spare room to Teresa. She said no, insisting she wanted to be near our mother. Secretly I was relieved. I had never liked Teresa or her thieving ways.

Little was expected of me by then, other than a monthly phone call and a yearly visit. It was December again when I called home to tell them that I couldn't make it home for Christmas. Yvonne answered the phone. "Where's Mama?" I asked.

"She been in the hospital for a week," she said.

"Why hasn't anyone called me?"

"Ain't nothing you can do about it way up there in Las Vegas," she said.

"In the first place, she's my mama too, and in the second

place, Las Vegas ain't way up there. It's only a few hours away," I said. I was so angry that I slammed the phone down without saying goodbye. I had some vacation time coming to me, and I convinced my boss that I needed to use it to go to L.A. I got a flight out, rented a car, and drove straight to the hospital.

The white hospital corridors seemed like one long hallway leading nowhere. I marched up to the nurses' station and asked for Sarah Gordon.

The nurse looked up from her paperwork. Her smile faded as she took me in—breathing hard, shaking, and sweating. "Are you okay?" she said.

My heart hammered in my ears as I attempted to speak. Is this what a heart attack feels like? I wondered, bracing myself on the counter. I counted to ten before I spoke. "I'm fine," I said. "I'm looking for Sarah Gordon's room. I'm her daughter."

"She's in room 428," the nurse said. "But visiting hours are not for another thirty minutes."

I started to argue, but I didn't think I had the strength. Sitting down on one of the hard plastic chairs, I began the busy work of biting my nails to the quick. I thought I could probably sneak in, but it wouldn't help if I were thrown out of the hospital for breaking the rules. Besides, I needed time to compose myself before seeing my mother. Although we had spoken by phone, I had not seen her in almost a year. No matter how she looked, I told myself, I was going to tell her that she looked great.

I was composed by the time the nurse said, "You can go in now."

I walked into room 428 and said, "Hi, Ma," in a cheerful voice.

My mother was a mess. Her hair, almost white now, stood out on her head like hairy icicles. With no makeup, she looked much older than her fifty-three years. I walked slowly toward her.

"Hey, Mary, when did you get here?" she asked.

"Just a little while ago. I'm on vacation," I said.

"You know they took my sister this morning," she said.

"Ma, Aint Dorothy died a long time ago."

"I know that, girl," she said. "I'm still at myself. I ain't nuts or nothing. I mean my spiritual sister. Jehovah made sure that I was sharing a room with another Witness. She died a few hours ago. Maybe I'll see her in the resurrection, if I'm blessed enough to be in God's memory."

That's the best she could hope for, I thought. According to my mother's belief, only 144,000 were sufficiently blessed to go to heaven. The rest of the God-fearing people had to hope they would be resurrected to a paradise on earth, where they would live forever and grow to perfection.

"How long you out here for?" she asked.

"Just a few days, then I have to get back to work," I said.

"You see Yvonne and them yet?"

"No, I came here right from the airport," I said.

"You flew!" my mother said. "You ain't never gonna get me up in no plane. If God wanted us to fly, he would have given us wings."

"Ma, it's no big deal. I've flown before. Remember when I went to London? That was the first time, and since then I've been all over the country on planes."

My mother sat up, then leaned back into her pillow with a sigh, as if the movement had required great effort.

Just then the hospital door flew open and Yvonne stepped in. "When did you get in, and why ain't you called?" she said to me.

I didn't get a chance to answer. Yvonne's thoughts were as unfocused as her eyes. Turning to my mother, she said, "Ma, you gotta talk to Teresa. She won't get no job, and she eating up all my food."

Before my mother could reply, I said, "Yvonne, Mama is sick and I know she don't want to talk about this stuff right now."

Ignoring me, Yvonne said, "It ain't just Teresa. It's Cynthia, too. She been staying at my house since you went into the hospital, and she ain't paying the bills at your house like you told her to."

"Yvonne, can I talk to you outside?" I asked.

Yvonne looked up as if she suddenly realized that I was still there and followed me into the hallway.

"What the hell are you doing in there?" I demanded, trying to keep my voice down. "That's a sick woman in there and she don't need to hear yo' bullshit. Are you high?"

"I'm trying to let Mama know what's going on in her house," Yvonne said. "And just 'cause you went to college don't mean you can talk crazy to me!"

I heard my mother's voice calling from the hospital room. "Y'all stop fighting out there," she said.

"My daddy drove me up here and he waiting for me outside," Yvonne said. "I don't have time for this bullshit."

Yvonne had lost a lot of weight in the months since I had last seen her. She wore her hair in long woven French braids that Bobby called tentacles. She was wearing hot-pink spandex and a hot-pink halter top that barely covered her large breasts. Her flip-flops made a sound like applause as she marched down the corridor and out of the nearest exit.

"She's like the Terminator," Morris had once said of Yvonne. "She can't be bargained with, she can't be reasoned with, and she doesn't feel pity or remorse, and absolutely will not stop until you are dead."

I shook my head and I went back into my mother's room. "Where Yvonne at?"

"She said her father was waiting for her or something," I said. "She had to go. Ma, what can I do?"

My mother looked up at the ceiling and said, "I didn't expect to live in Satan's system forever," she said. "I might see the New Order. You know that we living in the last days and this is the end of Satan's system of things."

It had become increasingly difficult to talk with my

mother without ending up in an argument about religion, so I didn't say anything. She was back with the Witnesses and that was that. "You got to make sure everybody is okay," she said. "When I'm gone, y'all gonna need each other." I shook my head at the thought. "I guess maybe your heart has been hardened like Pharaoh's," she said.

"Ma, please."

"Now you may be smart, but you ain't smarter than the greatest man that ever lived, Jesus Christ," she said. "He could see the good even in whores and tax collectors."

"Yeah, but those people repented," I said.

"Only Jehovah knows if a person is really repentant," my mother said. "Leave God's things to God. You just concentrate on having more love for people and more patience. They can do better if you give them a chance."

I didn't have a chance to respond. The door swung open, and in came five of my siblings, followed by a nurse who said there were too many people in the room. I left first. I peeled out of the hospital parking lot as if the police were after me. I detested rap music but I turned it up loud in the rental car; "911 Is a Joke" by Public Enemy blared from the speakers of the Ford Escort. I cranked up the A/C, although it was about seventy degrees outside. I finally turned it off when my teeth started to rattle. I wanted to be uncomfortable. I wanted to give my system a shock. Driving too fast down a desert highway, listening to bad music, and freezing my ass off felt akin to giving myself a good hard shake.

In college I had learned about survivor's guilt. People who survived war frequently felt guilty and suffered from nightmares and mood swings because they lived while others had not.

A family friend had once told me to put as many emotional resources into my family as I did into my education and career. I told him that I had, but my efforts hadn't done any good. I told him I felt like a person who had survived a shipwreck by climbing into a life raft. And there were others in the water, but whenever I tried to pull them onto the raft, they tried to pull me into the water.

Was I experiencing a mood swing? To be sure, I was. But it was more than that. This went beyond textbooks. This was a form of post-traumatic stress syndrome. I was escaping. I was escaping the madness of South Central L.A., my mother's hospital room, and my siblings. If I stayed longer, I would do what my mother asked. I would forgive them, even Yvonne. I would offer to come home and organize my mother's house until she recovered.

"No, no, and hell no," I said, jamming the palm of my hand against the steering wheel.

Or maybe I should stay, I thought. My mother needed me. I couldn't let my mother think of me as a cruel and hard-hearted pharaoh. I told myself that I would drive to the airport to exchange my ticket for a later flight. I could help out around the house, just until my mother got better. I had planned to stay in L.A. for only a few days, but I had accrued four weeks of vacation.

I didn't turn off for the airport, however. I got on the interstate and headed east. I just kept driving. The landscape flew by, from city to country to desert. In just a few hours I was back in Las Vegas.

When all was said and done, I just couldn't do it, not even for my mother. I couldn't get pulled into the water. My raft was getting out of my mother's house at eighteen—away from all of the madness.

FIFTEEN

The Beneficiary

Two weeks after returning to Las Vegas I received a call from my brother Morris.

"I cain't talk long," he whispered into the phone. "But Ma died a few days ago. They told me not to call you, but I thought you should know." I dropped the phone and sank to the floor. I could hear Morris on the other end. "Hello, hello, hello?" Finally, his voice was replaced by a beeping noise like an insistent alarm clock. I stared at the receiver, then kicked away the phone. I don't know how long I sat like that.

Somehow I was able to get into battle mode. I called my supervisor at work and told him I would need bereavement leave. I threw clothing into a duffel bag. A flight would be a waste of money, and I suspected I would need every nickel in Los Angeles. I could have driven my old Plymouth, but it would eat up in gas about as much as a flight would cost. The only other option was the bus.

I arrived at the Greyhound bus station ticket counter exactly forty minutes after hearing the news of my mother's death.

"I need a ticket to Los Angeles," I said to the clerk, a small Mexican man with a mustache that drooped over the sides of his mouth like a caterpillar on the move.

"What?"

"I need to get to L.A. right away," I said. "It's an emergency."

"Whatever," the clerk said.

"Look, my mother just died," I said.

"You can't make the bus go faster than the speed limit,

and then there's stops in between. It takes as long as it takes. That'll be thirty dollars."

He slid my ticket across the counter and yelled "next" all in one smooth movement.

Jesus, not even an I'm sorry, I thought. I had never quite understood that phrase that people toss at the grieving. I mean it's not as if they had anything to do with the death. Still, he could have at least given me that much.

I sat on a plastic chair and tried to read the schedule that was clicking by overhead. The bus trip would take seven hours. I folded my arms and closed my eyes against the welling tears.

"Excuse me," a woman said. "I was standing behind you in line."

Here it comes, I thought. A stranger who is going to tell me how sorry she was for the death of my mother. I looked up and a tall white lady in blue jeans and a red sweater was standing in front of me. Silver hoop earrings peeked out from her long red hair.

"Yes?" I said.

"Your shirt is on backwards and inside out," she said.

"Look, my mother just died," I said. I didn't care how my shirt looked, and who in the hell was she to tell me that it didn't look right?

The woman tossed back her red tresses and flounced away. A stray thought occurred to me: no girl could flounce like a white girl. We Black girls had the "sister neck," where our heads could swivel 180 degrees, but the white girl was the queen of the flounce.

I'd just shared my grief with two strangers who couldn't have cared less. Was this how it was going to be? People treating me as if nothing had happened? For me a crater had opened up beneath my feet and swallowed me whole, but no one cared. My tragedy doesn't mean shit to anybody else, I thought.

Yet I thought I somehow deserved this lack of compassion.

I needed to suffer. Why hadn't I stayed with my mother, those weeks ago, when she had needed me most? Would she still be alive? I could have taken some of the burden from her, I thought. I could have gone home and made sure the bills were paid and the house was clean by the time she got home from the hospital.

Head down, I slogged to the bus, passing my duffel to the driver, who tossed it into the holding compartment. My Sony Walkman was still in the duffel, and it crossed my mind to ask him to be careful with my bag. I realized, however, that I didn't care if my Walkman was smashed to smithereens. I'd brought it to listen to books on tape during the drive to L.A., but now I felt that I didn't deserve to be entertained on the way to my mother's funeral.

I shuffled to the back of the bus in order to be near the bathroom, which was the worst seat. I knew from previous experience that by the time we reached L.A., it would smell of pine cleaner, urine, and feces. That's okay, I thought, taking the window seat. I deserved it. I needed to suffer.

The red-haired woman, who had earlier notified me of my inside-out shirt, climbed the stairs into the bus. "Thanks for waiting," she said cheerily to the driver.

"I ain't waiting," he said. "We don't leave for another ten minutes."

"Okay," she said breathlessly. "Thanks anyway." She huffed her way to the back of the bus. "Is this seat taken?" she asked me.

I rolled my eyes and crossed my arms. I clucked my teeth and looked out the window. I sensed that she was going to make this trip even more wearisome for me, but it's what I deserved. She sat down.

"Do you mind?" she said, lifting her long hair out to me. One of her hoop earrings was caught in her hair, and she couldn't quite reach the clasp. The side of her pink face was two inches from me. I untangled her hair from her earring and popped the clasp. She removed the jewelry and then sat back with a sigh, like a contented dog with a scratched belly.

"I'm sorry about back there," she said.

"What?"

"I was going to tell you that I heard what you said about your mother, and I wanted to tell you that I was sorry, but then I started talking about your shirt being on wrong," she said. "That happens to me sometimes. I go to say one thing and something entirely different pops out. It's like some weird Tourettes or something. And I get embarrassed, and then I walk away, and I never say the thing I wanted to say in the first place. I'm glad we have some time together, so I can tell you how really sorry I am."

"It's all right," I said, staring out the window as the bus coughed to life. I wished that I had my Walkman, so I could tune her out.

"No, no, it's not all right," she said. "I lost my dad a few years ago. I wanted to tell you that from now on, it's never going to be all right again. You can wait forever trying to get over it."

Great! I thought. She's telling me I'll never get past this pain, that I would be miserable for another forty years, if I was lucky. I didn't say anything and she didn't really expect me to talk. She barely took a breath between sentences. She babbled on as we rode across the desert, stopping at little towns to pick up and drop off other travelers. I heard about how she grew up in Thousand Oaks, and how she wanted to be an actress, and how everyone told her she looked like Lucille Ball, and how her first boyfriend was "way into redheads" but refused to marry her. She even talked to me through the closed bathroom door while she was sitting on the toilet. It's okay, I thought. This is what I deserved. I had refused to save my mother or even make her last days comfortable.

As the bus lurched into the station, the woman jumped up as if there was a trampoline under her seat and she trotted to the front of the bus ahead of everyone.

"Take care. It was nice talking to you," she said, and she was out the door.

I couldn't get up. It was as if someone were holding me down. Maybe if I just waited, I would wake up and discover this had all been a nightmare.

Get your butt off this bus, Mary, I told myself. After sitting for ten minutes on the now-empty bus, I got off. My duffel had been tossed on the curb and the cargo-hold door had been shut. The driver stood next to the front of the bus, smoking a cigarette and looking annoyed.

I picked up my duffel and went into the station, amazed to see my brother Morris coming toward me. He threw his arms around me.

"When did you get here?" I asked. "How did you know I would be on that bus?"

"When your phone line went dead, I just called the bus station in Las Vegas, and I knew you would be on the next thing smokin'. You're kinda predictable, Mare," he said, using his old pet name for me.

I preferred dependable, but I didn't say so. I deserved to be insulted, I thought. That's me: Old Predictable Mary with a dead mother.

"I'll carry your bag, Mare," Morris said. "I ain't got no car, but I can carry your bag on the bus."

"Sure," I said. "What happened, Morris? I mean I just talked to Ma a little while ago. She said she was feeling better."

"Mama died in the hospital, and then Yvonne started going all crazy about how she was the beneficiary of the insurance, because she was the oldest girl," he said. "They told me not to call you, but I thought you deserved to know."

"Where's Ma now?"

"She at some funeral home that Yvonne sent her to," Morris said. "I don't know where. Everything is all mixed up at home, and people just sitting around crying."

I was shocked that he didn't know where my mother's

body had been sent. My siblings had never cared much for organizational details, and I knew that the grief had sidelined even the sturdiest of them. They had left my mother's body in the care of my manic-depressive sister, Cynthia, and my crack-head sister, Yvonne. It was a real fuster cluck. Still, I couldn't resist asking another direct question.

"Why didn't they want you to call me?" I asked.

"I don't know," he said. "Yvonne kept saying stuff like they would probably invite you to the funeral but you cain't do nothing way up there in Las Vegas. But Ma been dead for three days, and nobody is making no funeral arrangements that I can see, so I called you."

"Thanks for that," I said.

Morris was only two years younger than me, but he seemed like a child. At twenty-three he still lived at home, collected comic books, and talked on the phone with his friends for hours each night. With a sister's eye, I could see that he was good-looking. He was almost six foot, and he had a beautiful curly afro and light brown skin that gave him an almost Arab appearance. His face was perfectly symmetrical like Denzel Washington's and he had a Kirk Douglas dimple in his chin. He also had three day's growth of beard, and his soft brown eyes were bloodshot, probably from crying.

I decided on another direct question. "How are things?"

"People been dropping by all week and asking about the funeral. Some of them said they dropped money by Yvonne's house," he said.

Those people were probably from the neighborhood, I thought. They were engaging in the time-honored tradition of the poor helping to bury one another. Flowers were not usually sent to grieving families in South Central, but dribs and drabs of cash were common. When they didn't have money, neighbors brought over a covered dish.

Morris and I boarded the RTD bus. I took the window seat and Morris sat beside me. I took his hand and we sat silently in our mutual grief. I peered out of the window at the passing landscape of downtown Los Angeles. There seemed to be more high-rises than I remembered. At two a.m. the streets were almost empty, which seemed odd coming from Las Vegas, where there was action twenty-four-seven. A few bums slept in doorways, but otherwise the city had the dingy, deserted appearance of an urban ghost town.

I leaned my head against the glass and tried to sleep. As I closed my eyes, I remembered Ma. On my first day of school at Head Start, my mother told me that we were going to fly there. In the front yard of the school, my mother asked, "Ready for takeoff?" She counted down from ten, and then she grabbed me by my arms and spun me around in a circle. We laughed and laughed, until we both collapsed to the ground. I told her I felt dizzy, and she hugged me to her large chest. I felt exactly as a nesting bird must feel—safe, right, and sure. I don't know why this particular memory elbowed its way into my thoughts that night on the bus, but it brought a tightness to my chest and tears to my eyes.

The bus stopped not far from my mother's house. Inside, Teresa—now nineteen years old—hugged me. I hugged her back and then got right to business.

"Where's Mama's body?" I asked.

"Yvonne doin' the 'rangements," Cynthia said from the couch. "She say she is listed as the beneficiary in the insurance."

"I'm gonna need Yvonne's phone number," I said.

Cynthia wrote it down on a piece of notebook paper and handed it to me. There was no dial tone on the wall phone.

"What happened to the phone?" I asked.

"It's been cut off for a week," Cynthia said.

Teresa walked with me to the phone booth on our street corner, and I dialed Yvonne's number.

"What?" Yvonne finally asked, picking up the phone after fifteen rings.

"Yvonne, this is Mary," I said. "I'm in town. Where is Mama's body?"

"She be at Coroner Johnson," she said, slurring her words.

Damn, I thought. Yvonne was not sober.

"I'm da beneficiary. And I'm gonna be doin' the 'range-ments," Yvonne said.

"I know," I said, through clenched teeth. "I'm here to help."

"Don't nobody need your fucking help," she snapped, hanging up before I could get another word in.

I thumbed through the Yellow Pages, looking for Coroner Johnson's funeral home.

There were no listings for Coroner Johnson. I called 411, but the operator told me there were no listings for a business with that name. It was hot in the tiny glass room. I had closed the accordion door, and now I peered through the glass at Teresa who was hugging herself against the cool of the night. I rested my forehead against the cool glass wall. I needed to clear my thoughts.

My mother had been informed of her mother's death in a phone booth, she had told me. It was 1964, and she had been pregnant with me at the time. Her mother had been in the hospital for a week. A nurse came on the line, saying, "Oh, that one. She died last night." My mother stood in that phone booth for hours, convinced that her mother would be dead only if she stepped outside the phone booth. I had always found this a curious story until that moment, that night, when I myself was grappling with the death of my mother. I don't know how long I stood there with my head against the glass. I heard the scraping of the door on the concrete.

"Come on, Mary," Teresa said, taking my arm and leading me out of the phone booth. "You ain't gonna find it."

At my mother's house I decided to put on my investigator's hat. My mother's bed was unmade. The six-drawer chest was missing two drawers, and papers spilled out onto the floor. I found my mother's phone book, the words brothers and sisters scribbled on the cover—my mother's Jehovah's Witness friends. In the corner phone booth, I dug deep into

my bag, looking for the twenty quarters I had won from a
Las Vegas slot machine the week before. I had tossed them
in my bag without thinking. At least one thing was going my
way. I started dialing numbers.

Most numbers were disconnected. My mother had been
back with the Witnesses for only a few years. Clearly this was
an old book. On the tenth number, a woman answered the
phone.

"Is this Sister Regent?" I asked.

"Yes."

"This is Mary Hill. I'm sorry to call so early in the morning. My mother is Sarah Gordon."

"Oh, that's all right. I'm so sorry to hear about Sister
Gordon," she said. "When is the service?"

"That's just it, Sister Regent," I said. "I'm doing the funeral arrangements, and I don't know where the hospital has
sent my mother's body." I didn't mention the fact that none
of my siblings seemed to know the location of my mother's
body. "Is there someplace that the Witnesses use?" I asked.

"Oh yes," she said. "We use the Conner-Johnson Funeral
Home on Avalon. Let me get you the number."

Of course, it was Conner-Johnson and not Coroner
Johnson. The coroner wouldn't be involved in a death inves-
tigation unless foul play was suspected, which I well knew
from my years as a police reporter.

The sun was just coming up and the streetlights started
to wink off. I realized that Conner-Johnson's Funeral Home
would not be open for another few hours. Suddenly I felt
very tired and, mission accomplished, I returned home.

Only Cynthia was up, lounging on the couch as she stared
blankly at the test pattern on the TV. Fred slumped to her
left, and Little Sarah, her daughter, snuggled to her right.
Both were sleeping, which meant my mother's bed was free.
As long as I could remember, my mother usually had some
toddler sleeping with her in her bed. And if not the toddler,
the most recent father of the latest toddler.

The citrusy scent of Jean Naté, my mother's favorite fragrance, filled the room. My mother had been allergic to the citrus in the fragrance, but she used the perfume anyway because one of us kids had bought it for her.

I didn't want to be disturbed, so I shoved a kitchen chair under the knob to jam it shut.

Leafing through the papers on the floor, I found bills from the electric company, the landlord, and the gas and water companies. None of the envelopes had been opened. A savings passbook from Bank of America showed exactly twelve dollars in my mother's bank account.

Among the papers was a letter, which read:

To my children:

Now that I am gone, I'll leave you all with these words. I loved you. I hope I was there when you needed me but now God has taken me and I'm at rest. Whatever you pursue in life, please try to do your very best. Without me to push you to go forth, I hope with all my heart and soul that you remember what you were taught and seek another's hand to hold.

It was signed Mama.

The letter was dated six months before my mother's death. Tears filled my eyes again, but this time I let them flow as I hugged the letter to my chest.

Among the papers I also found my mother's insurance policy from the Pierce National Life Insurance Company. She had paid a monthly premium of $27.46 for many years. The policy covered only the cost of burial. I was listed as the primary beneficiary, with Cynthia listed as contingent, a provision that had been in place for the last six years.

I crawled into my mother's bed and cried myself to sleep.

The next morning I was awakened by hammering on the door. I looked wildly around a room that I didn't recognize. I discovered that my clothes were wet. Had it been raining the previous night? Had the sprinkler system gone off in some hotel where I was staying? Was there a fire? Exactly what was going on?

Then, I heard Willie's voice, "Open this damn door, Mary!"

That's right, I thought. I am home. I am in my dead mother's bedroom. I went to the door, removed the chair, and opened the door.

"I need a gun," Willie said. He wore a long black trench coat with black sweatpants and a black T-shirt with a skull design. His belly bulged out from the bottom of the shirt, which made the skull look like was as if it were chomping down on a loaf of freshly baked bread.

"What exactly do you need a gun for?" I asked, glancing at the trunk, where I knew my mother had kept her arsenal.

"I'm gonna kill that doctor that killed my mother," he said. "Call me 'The Punisher.'"

That's it! I almost shouted, recognizing his outfit now. He was dressed as his favorite comic book antihero, a vigilante called "The Punisher."

"Willie, The Punisher is a comic-book character and not a real person," I said evenly. "What makes you think the doctor killed Ma?"

"Mama said he was giving her the wrong medicine," Willie said.

"Boy, you want to go to jail?" I said. "There are ways to deal with stuff like this, and shooting the doctor ain't it. We could get a lawyer or something. We could get an autopsy to see exactly what killed her."

Morris stepped into the room, taking Willie by the arm. "Willie, be reasonable," he said. "You know The Punisher only did what he did because he got poisoned with some drugs that made him crazy. Let Mary handle this stuff her way."

"She got till the end of the week, and then somebody gonna get punished," Willie said, and left the room with a dramatic sweep of his long black trench coat.

Oh, brother, I thought. "Thanks, Morris," I told him. "I'm glad you speak comic book."

My mother's steamer trunk was locked.

"Do you know where Ma keeps the key to the trunk, Morris?"

"Nope, your guess is as good as mine," he replied.

I looked in all of her last-known hiding places: under the mattress, where my mother used to stash cash and important papers; in the space heater in the floor; in a vase of silk flowers on her dresser. Then, finally, I found it under a bedside lamp.

I opened the steamer trunk and found all her guns and knives.

"I'm going to have to get rid of these," I told Morris.

"Come on, Mare," he protested. "You have to leave us at least one. This is a rough neighborhood. What if Bobby comes back around?"

I took the .38-caliber out of the trunk. My mother kept her guns loaded. I removed the bullets and handed the weapon to Morris.

For the next few hours, a friend drove me to several pawnshops in the neighborhood. I didn't want to haggle. I just wanted the weapons out of the house. In the end, there was about $350 to put toward the funeral.

I called the Conner-Johnson Funeral Home and asked about the cost of the funeral. A receptionist told me to expect a bill for about $3,500, with $600 upfront. I paid $643 to the funeral home, and I paid $862.93 for an autopsy. My mother's body was transferred to the morgue downtown. The funds in my bank account—which contained my life's savings of a few thousand dollars—was rapidly dwindling.

The report came back seventy-two hours later, listing the cause of death as natural, brought on by a pulmonary thromboembolism with a contributing cause of hypertensive cardiovascular disease.

The report referenced her complaint, upon admission to the hospital, of blood clots in her legs and feet. Several tests were done, and she was given blood-thinning medication.

Apparently the clots moved, lodging in her lungs. A drain tube inserted in her left side accidentally punctured her lung. Her lung was repaired, and she was told that she would be able to go home in two days. Forty-eight hours later, she was pronounced dead.

I photocopied the autopsy report and my mother's last letter for each of my siblings. I asked Cynthia to mail copies of the report and the letter to Yvonne.

That night, I met with the family for the last time.

"The funeral home works with Jehovah's Witnesses, so they said we can have the service at the Kingdom Hall, and they will wait for the insurance to pay the balance for the funeral. There's no cost for the service because she was a member of the congregation. We're going to have the funeral this weekend," I announced.

"Are you gonna sue that doctor, Mary?" Cynthia asked.

"I don't know if there's any cause when the autopsy report that I gave you says Mama's death was due to natural causes," I said. "It says her lung was punctured by mistake, but it was mostly natural causes that killed her. Y'all know she was sick for a long time. So I think we need to get off this lawsuit thing, and we need to start focusing on the household finances and the custody of the minors."

Everyone stared at me blankly.

"Maybe we should think about foster homes," I said. "Children under eighteen need to have a legal guardian to go to the doctor or school or whatever."

"If you put my brothers and sister in a foster home and something happens to them, I'm gonna find you and kill you," Willie said.

"Yeah, I know because you're The Punisher," I said, with withering sarcasm.

Willie had never had a job in his life but referred to walking my little brother and niece to school every day as his "job." My mother used to give him an allowance of ten dollars a week for this task. It had taken him an entire year to save two hundred dollars, after his daily expenses of comic books, sweets, and the occasional Blockbuster movie rental.

"Willie, think about it," I told him gently. "You can't even take care of yourself. Do you really think you can take care of little kids?"

"I can do it if I win the lottery," Willie said.

"Willie, you don't even play the lottery," I shot back.

"Why don't you come back and run the house, Mare?" Morris said finally.

"Because I don't want to," I said. "I have a life in Las Vegas, and I need to get back to it."

Truthfully my life in Las Vegas wasn't so grand. I hated my boss, and I found the politics at my paper too small-town for my taste. I had been planning to move to another paper before my mother died. But my family didn't need to know all that. There was already enough uncertainty in their lives.

"Anybody else willing to take custody?" I asked.

My sixteen-year-old brother Mark raised his hand.

"That's sweet, Mark, but it has to be someone over eighteen," I said.

Then Teresa, who was nineteen and fresh out of jail, said "I'll do it."

I threw my arm around Teresa's shoulder and guided her out to the porch.

"That's great, Teresa, but I want you to know that I found a pile of bills in Mama's bedroom," I said. "If it becomes too much, call me. I'll come and get you and the little kids. Okay?"

She nodded.

I went to the printer's and had obituaries printed, reading it through again on the yellow printer paper.

> And God Himself will be with them. And he will wipe out every tear from their eyes, and death will be no more, neither will mourning nor outcry nor pain be anymore. The former things have passed away.

On January 21, 1937, a daughter was born to the union of Dorothy May Reed and John Wilbur Gordon Sr. in Alexandria, Louisiana. Sarah believed in God and the Jehovah's Witness persuasion from age of eleven until the time of her death.

She was the mother of eleven children: Steven, Yvonne, Bobby, Cynthia, Mary, Morris, Willie, Teresa, Mariah, Mark, and Fred.

She was the grandmother of three: Everett Doss, Tamie Doss, and Sarah Newhouse.

She received her education in Los Angeles, California. She went to school in the Los Angeles Unified School District and received a high school diploma from Jordan High School, then went to Compton Junior College, where she obtained an Associate in Arts degree.

In the end I decided not to include our various last names in the obituary. Our motley assortment of fathers was not something that bound us together; it was my mother and her boundless love.

Epilogue

Cynthia called me two months after the funeral and asked if I would give her a few hundred dollars for a new apartment. She and my other siblings had been evicted from my mother's house. I sent the money through Western Union. I assumed they received it. I never heard from Cynthia again. In fact, most of my siblings did not speak to me again, with a few notable exceptions.

A few months after my mother's death, Teresa called me to rescue her, along with two of my mother's minor children, Mariah and Fred.

I was reminded of advice from a family friend who said that I was, metaphorically, on a raft, and I had an obligation to pull as many of my mother's other children onto that raft as possible to keep them from drowning.

"I will," I responded. "But I will have to let some go, if they threaten to drown me too."

So, I agreed to take in Teresa, Mariah, and Fred, with the caveat that Teresa would take custody of Mariah and Fred within the next year. If she agreed to that, all three could live with me, and I would teach Teresa everything I knew about finding a decent place to live, getting and keeping a job, and staying on the right side of the law.

Teresa and I had many late-night discussions about such things. She told me that she had learned her lesson about living outside the law and did not want to return to jail. "I don't want to give anyone the power to tell me when to get up, when to go to bed, and when to take a shit," she said.

My mother was right again, I thought. Prison rehabilitation was possible.

I remembered part of my mother's last letter to us:

To my children…Without me to push you to go forth, I hope with all my heart and soul that you remember what you were taught and seek another's hand to hold. It was signed: Mama.

I was determined to honor my mother's last request. Teresa needed to work in order to fulfill her part of the bargain. I showed her how to apply for jobs. A short time later, a friend at the newspaper told me that her roommate needed to hire a hostess for a Las Vegas Denny's restaurant. I volunteered Teresa. She got the job and worked hard. True to her word, she took custody of Mariah and Fred and within a year moved into their own place in Las Vegas.

I rented another apartment—a one-person studio.

Finally, after so many years, I had my own raft and some measure of peace. And I was left with the gratitude for the woman who taught me to love hard—my mama.

ACKNOWLEDGMENTS

As I began to write these acknowledgments, I couldn't help but think of all those prize fighters who thank the Lord for helping them knock the hell out of some guy. That said, I would like to thank the Mighty God Jehovah for His many blessings, including my mother. I am grateful to my mother for leading such an extraordinary life that I was compelled to write it down.

I want to thank the Santa Barbara Writing Workshop and all those in the Pirate Workshops for listening to my drafts and giving me useful and heartfelt feedback. I would like to thank Andrea Somberg of Harvey Klinger for believing in this project. Foremost, I would like to thank my husband, Dr. Marcus Wagner, for putting up with me, and for supporting me when I decided to become a writer. Finally, I want to thank all those girls in the 'hood who bear up under tremendous odds in South Central Los Angeles. This book is for you.